When
RELAXATION IS HAZARDOUS TO YOUR HEALTH

Why We Get Sick *After* the Stress is Over and What You Can Do Now to Protect Your Health

By

MARC SCHOEN, Ph.D.

Mind Body Health Books

When
RELAXATION IS HAZARDOUS TO YOUR HEALTH

Why We Get Sick *After* the Stress is Over and What You Can Do Now To Protect Your Health

By

Marc Schoen, Ph.D.

Published by:
Mind Body Health Books (SAN 253-9020)
P.O. Box 8579
Calabasas, CA 91372
U.S.A.

Copyright 2001 by Marc Schoen, Ph.D.
Library of Congress Cataloging-in Publication Data
Schoen, Marc
When Relaxation is Hazardous to Your Health
1,Health. 2, Self-Help. I Title
LCCN 2001117622
ISBN 0971117608

TABLE OF CONTENTS

ACKNOWLEDGMENTS

There have been many people central to the creation of this book. First and foremost, is my wife **Marlene**, who made this book possible in two huge ways. In reading every draft of this book, she offered many invaluable suggestions and ideas to improve the book. Second, through Marlene's endless emotional support, encouragement, understanding, and love, she made it possible for me to start and finish this book. Marlene – having you in my life is the best thing that ever happened to me.

My mother and father (Esther and Sy), who have never wavered in their love and support, and in coming through for me when I needed them. You have made so much possible for me and I am forever grateful. My two children, **Meriah and Nathan**, who have so easily assimilated Mind-Body techniques in their young lives, have inspired me to find ways to help others incorporate these tools in their lives. Their unconditional love has made me a better person and fostered a desire to make a difference in the world in a large way.

Jaci Schoen, of Just Designs, who I love as a sister and a friend, who was the creative force behind the book design and cover. Thank you Jaci for all your hard work. **Jeff Lerman,** who throughout the writing process, offered many helpful suggestions – thank you for your many thoughts and ideas.

My deep gratitude to **Steve Bing,** who believed in me and Mind-Body Medicine. Steve – your generosity and support has made a big difference for me and the future of Mind-Body Medicine. **Dr. Norman Stone,** who I relied on for his great intelligence and wisdom to find flaws and inconsistencies in my manuscript. Norm, your input was invaluable and made a big difference. **Dr. Ken Nowack,** who offered valuable suggestions and was the formative inspiration behind the concept of Delayed and Immediate Reactors. **Dr. John Milliman,** whose feedback was helpful throughout the book, but particularly influential in the chapter, "Let-Down in the Work

Place."

Jeff and Elizabeth Kramer, who took their time to read the book and offer their input and feedback. **Dr. William Deardorff**, who I greatly respect for his Health Psychology expertise and writing skills, took time out from his hectic schedule to offer suggestions and improvements for the book. **Dr. Steven Jacobs** for his input into how shifting activation levels leads to fatigue. Last and certainly not least, **Laurie Viera** who was very helpful in enhancing the readability of this book. Laurie, your excellent questions challenged me and helped create clarity and refinement of the book's concepts.

Disclaimer

The purpose of this book is to inform the reader about a syndrome (The Let-Down Effect) that has not been addressed previously and to offer tools that can be used to stop this syndrome. Every effort has been made to provide the reader with information that is based on current research and my twenty years of clinical experience. There is no intent to suggest that these tools are to be used in lieu of sound medical treatment, good nutrition, a healthy life style, and any other cogent health intervention. Instead, please view the information and tools offered as strategies that can be used in tandem with other accepted forms of health intervention. As a rule, the best health outcomes are often based on more than one health intervention modality. I encourage the reader to bring this information to your trusted health provider(s) and have him or her develop a sound strategy of incorporating these tools into your present health regimen.

Chapter 1

IN THE BEGINNING

For as long as I can remember, I have been interested in using the mind to positively affect the body. It became a driving force in my life. Ultimately, this passion led me to get my Ph.D. in Psychology, while specializing in Psychoneuroimmunology, which studies the relationship between the mind and body.

As a professor at the UCLA Medical School, a teacher of medical residents, a researcher, and a psychologist in private practice, I have had the opportunity to share my knowledge of Mind-Body Medicine with thousands of patients and hundreds of medical professionals.

One of the most surprising things I have discovered in my 20 years of working and doing research in the field of mind-body medicine is this: While it is well known in medicine that stress is hazardous to our health, what is less well known is that many of us do not begin suffering from stress-related illnesses until *after* the stress is over. Many of us get sick *after* we finish a demanding project at work, during or *after* we go on vacation, or *after* we retire from a lifetime of fast-paced living.

Does this mean that slowing down and relaxing is actually a hidden health hazard? The truth is that relaxation, like any prescription from our doctors, can only be an effective cure when taken in the right doses and at the right times.

This book will explore this fascinating mind-body phenomenon and show you how to balance your own times of stress and relaxation. What you will learn will enable you to make a positive difference in your health – quickly and easily.

Chapter 2

THE LET–DOWN EFFECT

All week long I kept fantasizing about how good it would feel when my wife and I arrived in Hawaii. I imagined myself absorbing the sun and tropical air as I relaxed and slept on a beautiful Maui beach. I worked extra long days that week so that I could leave for my vacation knowing that every problem had been solved and every important task completed. With everything handled, I just knew I could fully enjoy my upcoming getaway. On the night before my departure, I left my office with a sense of closure, but I still felt hyped- up and tense. I knew there would still be much to do when I got home. I am sure you know the drill.

After we finished our packing, we went to sleep late. The next day, we awakened early and dashed to the airport. The traffic was horrendous, and I felt anxious about making our flight.

After barely arriving in time, we checked our

bags and ran to the gate to board our plane. My heart was pounding and I had broken into a sweat. But I felt comforted knowing that when we ultimately landed in Hawaii I could at last relax and start my vacation. Finally, when on the plane, I began to slow down somewhat. But my relaxation was relatively contained, for I knew that there were still seven hours of flight time standing between me and fully letting go.

By the time we checked into our hotel, I could hear the ocean calling my name. Dropping everything in our room, we put on our bathing suits and hurried to the beach. We staked out the best place we could find, and I could already feel my guard starting to fall. The geared-up feeling was giving way to a more relaxed feeling, a heaviness in my limbs, a slight fatigue, and a dulling of my senses. I began to feel a little lightheaded and spacey. I assumed I was tired from the long haul to get here. Since, I was finally in Hawaii, I could fully let-down my guard and completely relax. Before, I knew it, I had fallen into a deep sleep.

I awakened to find that a dreadful thing had happened while I was sleeping: **I had become sick.** Somehow I had managed to develop a sore throat and ear ache. How could this be? Wasn't relaxing, sleeping, and being on vacation one of the best things I could do for my health? How was it that I had managed to remain healthy all year long, even though I was working hard and putting in long hours? And now, when I was doing all the right things, I got sick.

If the above scenario sounds familiar to you, then you are already acquainted with the Let-Down Effect and Let-Down-related illnesses.

The Let-Down Effect Can Affect Our Health in Many Other Situations..

Do you ever find yourself becoming ill:

* **after finishing a project at work or after completing school finals?**

* **after a stressful meeting?**

* **after returning from a vacation?**

* on the weekends?

* after a failure or frustrating experience?

* after having a conflict with another individual?

* after returning home from an exciting party, a social gathering, or a date?

* after completing a project or goal that has taken months or years to complete?

All of the above situations can lead to the Let-Down Effect and result in illness.

What is the Let-Down Effect?

The Let-Down Effect occurs when we suddenly shift from a very High Activation state (in which we feel high energy, great joy or pleasure, anger, aggravation, tension, or anxiety) to a Low Activation state (when we feel relaxed, quiet, calm, tired, or still). Due to this sudden shift, we become vulnerable to illness and symptoms.

States of High Activation can be either pleasant or stressful. Any situation that increases our internal

6

excitement can lead to a High Activation level.

Most people believe that illness generally occurs during the throes of stress or work. In actuality, one of our most vulnerable times for illness is the time **immediately** following periods of stress or work, when we are, in fact, able to let go and relax.

Why do I call this phenomenon the "Let-Down Effect?" When we relax, we let down our guard, that state of mental vigilance and high mental and physical activity we experience when we are in a stressful or exciting situation. Ironically, at the same time we **let down** our guard, the body's immune system is also **letting down** its guard. The term "let down" in our language is also associated with disappointment. What could be more of a let down than anticipating a relaxing break from the demands of work or coming home feeling euphoric after an exciting social event, only to come down with a cold or a headache as soon as we get fully relaxed?

The first time I became aware of the Let-Down

Effect was when I was in college going through my final exams. During exams, it was typical to sleep less, work late into the night, and eat poorly. The three Cs —candy, coffee, and chips were my basic staples. These conditions certainly were not health promoting.

Of course, my classmates and I were all determined to remain healthy. We just knew that becoming sick would be the kiss of death, for there would be no way to complete all the work we had to do. Yet we all felt we were teetering on the edge of a cold or flu. I remember promising myself that once finals were over, I would reward myself with plenty of sleep, exercise, and healthy food.

Fortunately, most of us remained healthy through finals. Yet several days after finals, while receiving plenty of sleep and eating healthy meals, the reaper of illness paid us a visit. Soon we were all falling victim to some form of sickness. The Let-Down Effect was alive and well.

After spoiling several vacations by becoming

sick, I was dead set on finding a solution to the Let-Down Effect. I was finished with sipping warm tea, taking aspirin, decongestants, and consuming tons of vitamin C when I should have been enjoying my holiday.

I began observing my patients and noticed a similar pattern in them as well. Many of my headache patients were not developing headaches in the throes of stress, but rather, once the stress was finished, such as at the end of their day or on the weekends. A similar pattern was apparent in my patients with skin disorders such as eczema or psoriasis, which manifests as itching, flaking, drying, or cracking skin. The pattern was most glaring in those who frequently developed upper respiratory infections, such as colds and sore throats.

Even autoimmune disorders such as rheumatoid arthritis, ulcerative colitis, multiple sclerosis, and lupus tended to have major flare-ups on the Let-Down side of stress. (By the way, an autoimmune condition is one in which the body's immune system actually attacks the body.) Chronic pain conditions such as back pain or fibromyalgia (a condition in which the body develops painful areas, such as the neck, shoulders, and back, often coupled with fatigue), also tended to worsen during the Let-Down phase.

I also noticed a Let-Down pattern in some recently retired patients. Many people who enjoy excellent health throughout their working lives, such as the hard-working executive who was a neighbor of mine, looked forward to retirement only to become ill shortly thereafter. I remember him often saying to me, "As soon as I retire, all I'm going to do is golf." He did finally retire, and three months later he had a stroke.

After observing the Let-Down Effect in so many of the patients who came to me for symptom improvement, I felt certain that it was not my problem alone. This gave me an even greater incentive to find a solution to Let-Down related illnesses. As a result, I developed simple techniques that have made a tremendous difference in my life and in the lives of my patients.

In this book, you will learn what you can do to stop Let-Down-related illnesses in your life. You will learn how to identify the Let-Down Effect when it is happening, and you will acquire tools that you can rapidly employ to turn it around and preserve your health. In following chapters you will discover simple techniques that you can easily learn and assimilate into your life. These tools can make a dramatic difference in reducing or stopping Let-Down related illnesses.

There is no longer any reason to feel at the mercy of your symptoms. Nor is there any reason that your symptoms should dictate when you can go out socially, travel, or enjoy a quiet evening at home. In just a few minutes each day, these tools can bring more health and happiness back into your life. And not only can you improve your health right now, you can also improve your chances of sustaining good health throughout your later years.

Chapter 2 Summary:

1. The Let-Down Effect is caused by a **rapid shift** from High Activation to Low Activation.

2. States of High Activation can be caused by either pleasurable or stressful situations.

3. Situations such as finishing a project, a stressful meeting, weekends, vacations, or interpersonal conflicts can set us up for the Let-Down Effect.

4. The Let-Down Effect can lead to or affect such conditions as headaches, skin disorders, autoimmune reactions, stomach disorders, chronic fatigue, and fibromyalgia.

Chapter 3

HOW THE LET DOWN EFFECT
LEADS TO ILLNESS

To fully understand how the Let-Down Effect leads to illness, we must first understand how stress, its precursor, impacts our health.

When we perceive a situation as stressful, the part of the brain that is responsible for emotion, the hypothalamus, releases a substance called a corticotropin releasing factor (CRF). This substance travels to the pituitary gland, which in turn releases corticotropin itself (ACTH).

ACTH then travels through the body until it reaches the adrenal glands. The adrenal glands respond to ACTH by releasing a type of a steroid called cortisol. These steroids are part of our instinctual "fight or flight" syndrome, and their function is to help mobilize the body's defenses.

The presence of these cortisol steroids in our

bodies is helpful during short bouts of stress and life-threatening situations. However, prolonged steroid levels can increase blood sugar, elevate blood pressure, and suppress the immune system. High chronic levels of these steroids directly accelerate the aging process, from shorter life spans, osteoporosis, heart disease, and muscle atrophy, to shrinkage of the brain.

Chronic stress and cortisol release have also been found to lower our natural pain coping substances, while elevating joint inflammation in the body. The result in such cases is chronic pain.

There is also growing evidence that chronic stress plays a part in autoimmune disorders, contributing to their onset and progression. In skin disorders, stress can affect the blood flow that nourishes the skin, as well as the immune response in the skin.

As you can see, the effects of chronic stress are pervasive.

You would expect that the body would be most susceptible to illness when it is at its most compromised point; that is, in the throes of stress, but this is not the case. Instead, **we are most vulnerable to illness when the stress has abated in our lives.** This paradox becomes the basis for the Let-Down Effect.

Darwin's theory of evolution may well provide some insight into this paradox. The human body has evolved throughout the years in a manner that provides the best chance of survival. Those humans who coped most effectively with danger in their environment without becoming ill were eventually those who survived the longest. Through this process, known as natural selection, the human body has evolved mechanisms that inhibit illness and pain during periods of sudden physical and emotional stress.

As I discussed previously, at the onset of stress the adrenal glands release steroids into the body. In response, the immune system releases cells called Natural Killer Cells, which are the immune system's first line of defense against infection. In addition, the body releases natural morphine-like substances called endorphins into the bloodstream. Endorphins can lower pain, while elevating mood. (This release of endorphins might, in part, account for the addictive nature of stressful, high-excitement modes of living in our modern world). Nevertheless, in the short term these mechanisms make it possible for individuals to endure amazing conditions while still functioning effectively and healthfully. It has been under these conditions that many individuals have performed in extraordinary and creative ways.

Unlike modern mankind, early man likely did not have to cope with chronic stress. Instead, he had to react to immediate danger. Chronic stress is a malady that applies to modern civilization. Although the Let-Down Effect is evidence that the human body has not yet evolved to the point where we can endure chronically stressful conditions, we can block Let-Down-related illnesses by adopting the tools I will outline in this book. Just as early man made an enormous leap toward a higher quality of life by discovering how to make and use physical tools from stone, we modern humans can raise our level of health and well being by employing these new tools of the mind.

We Are Relaxing Just To Make Ourselves Sick

Traditional theory suggests that if we are in the throes of stress or on the verge of becoming ill, it is important to create a state of relaxation. Intuitively we would think that by inducing rapid and deep relaxation, we are inhibiting our stress reaction while at the same time promoting a healing response.

Contrary to popular wisdom, **rapid relaxation** can lead to the promotion of illness in those individuals who are sensitive to the Let-Down Effect, rather than to health. The same individuals who come to their therapists and health providers to be relaxed, merely return home to become sick or develop physical symptoms. Those individuals on the verge of a sore throat or cold may find that the rapidly induced relaxation makes them more likely to develop an upper respiratory infection. Migraine sufferers who are on the threshold of developing a headache may very well find themselves decked by a migraine several hours after a relaxing treatment.

After observing the relationship between rapid relaxation and illness a number of times, I began asking my patients to observe the physical sensations and thoughts that accompanied their deep relaxation and preceded their illness. Most patients reported that they began to feel a heaviness or sluggishness, fatigue, spaciness or fogginess, a slowing down feeling, or a sinking feeling prior to becoming sick or symptomatic.

It then became apparent to me that by inducing deep relaxation in these individuals as suggested by conventional wisdom, we were instead **creating the identical physical sensations that either precipitate or accompany illness.** Deep relaxation was placing these individuals into a state of Low Activation, which in turn created the Let-Down Effect and made them more vulnerable to illness. Without knowing it, we have been marching these individuals into the jaws of illness.

But Isn't Relaxation Supposed to be Healthy?

Relaxation itself is not the problem. Numerous studies attest that relaxation contributes to good health. When relaxation can be hazardous to our health is when we **suddenly shift** to a relaxed state after having been in a state of High Activation. To avoid the Let-Down Effect, therefore, it is necessary to **gradually shift** from a High Activation state to a relaxed or Low Activation state.

A popular misconception is that the Low Activation state is infinitely more healthy than the High Activation state. Although chronic High Activation or stress is clearly not healthy for the mind and the body, chronic Low Activation is not universally healthy either. In fact, some studies have suggested that chronic Low Activation makes us more vulnerable to illness. Yet many people have come to believe as fact that merely creating a relaxation response in the body promotes healing.

My clinical experience suggests something different. I have found that our minds begin to associate certain situations with health and others with illness, and that our bodies follow suit. For example, being with loving and nurturing friends may create a moderate state of activation that is far more conducive to good health than merely inducing a state of relaxation while we are at work. Therefore, we can best enhance our health by creating activation states that our bodies and minds associate with health, rather than creating relaxation alone.

When I began instructing my patients in how to alter their Low Activation states that typically preceded their illnesses and symptoms, they were able for the first time to stop the development of their symptoms.

So what is it about sudden deep relaxation in the body that promotes illness?

Earlier, I talked about how the release of cortisol steroids by our adrenal glands during extreme stress leads to the immune system's release of Natural Killer cells throughout the body. These soldiers of the immune system fortify the body by beefing up its defenses against infection. Once the hormonal stress signals cease, however, the number and activity of these immune soldiers begin to significantly drop in the blood stream. As a result, our immune defenses are thinned, leaving us more vulnerable to the very illnesses that they have so effectively been able to defend against. The very processes in the body that have allowed us to resist pain and illness during stress periods, ultimately shift to leave us wide open to illness.

Up to this point, stress hormones and endorphins have masked our fatigue and kept the body in a more activated state. When this High Activation ceases, the body begins to slow, and feelings of fatigue and exhaustion begin to unfold. This is the beginning of the Let-Down Effect. From a mental standpoint, we perceive ourselves as letting go or relaxing. But from a physical point of reference, we are actually shifting from a state of High activation to a state of Low Activation, and from a state of an immune system alert to an immune system collapse.

We can also understand the Let-Down Effect with the help of a metaphor drawn from *Star Trek*. In *Star Trek*, the good guys aboard the U.S.S. Enterprise would raise the shields on the spaceship when under attack by an alien vessel. These shields would protect the spaceship from incoming warheads. If the attack posed a serious threat to the spaceship, the shields were raised to Stage 4. Normally, the ship kept its shields at Stage 1, to ward off surprise and less serious threats. Raising the shields to Stage 4 required a tremendous amount of energy, which would have to be diverted from other centers of the spaceship. A prolonged use of the shields had damaging effects on the spaceship. To limit the damage and drain on the ship's energy supplies, and to enable the ship to replenish itself, the shields were rapidly dropped to stage 0 as soon as the attack was finished. However, by dropping the shields completely to Stage 0 (instead of the usual Stage 1), it now became vulnerable to other threats that were lurking near or around it.

In a similar manner, when we are under stress, our body mobilizes our defenses and raises our shields to a Stage 4. A sustained use of Stage 4 fatigues and depletes our body. If, after the stressful situation has passed, we **rapidly shift** to a state of relaxation, then our shields fall to a Stage 0. This is the essence of the Let-Down Effect. In this weakened state, our defenses are compromised, and we are less able to defend against any invading threat to our health.

Despite the mind making a distinction between relaxation and vulnerability, the body does not make this distinction. The body experiences both relaxation and vulnerability as letting down or letting go. Several studies have revealed that when we let go and accept the verdict of a terminal illness, we typically fare much worse than if we are determined to not give into the illness. By experiencing **sudden deep relaxation**, we are in essence letting go to any bacteria or viral condition that may have found its way into our system.

How Does the Shift from High Activation to Low Activation Lead to a Feeling of Fatigue?

During stressful or High Activation periods, our bodies also release high quantities of sugar the bloodstream, resulting in higher blood glucose levels. The body converts this extra sugar into the energy we need to cope with the situation that is causing our High Activation state. When the stressful period ends, the glucose levels begin to drop, leaving us feeling sluggish, fatigued, and spacey.

Additionally, while our bodies are in the throes of stress, our cells become accustomed to absorbing and receiving greater quantities of steroids and endorphins.

After a period of sustained absorption, our system begins to require greater quantities of these hormones to create the desired effect. This process is akin to drug addiction. Over time, drug addicts need higher quantities of a drug to create the same effect that smaller quantities had previously produced.

Once the body shifts from this period of elevated activation, the level of these stress hormones drops drastically. The combined effect of the body becoming accustomed to receiving more of these steroids, while at the same time shutting down its supply of them, places us in a state of withdrawal. As a result, we feel depleted and exhausted.

Now that I have explained how the Let-Down Effect works to create illness, the next step will be to pinpoint your own degree of susceptibility to this phenomenon.

Chapter 3 Summary:

1. Many individuals are most vulnerable to illness after the stress has abated in their lives.

2. The body has evolved the means of activating our immune system during acute, sudden stress, but has not yet learned to cope on its own with chronic periods of stress.

3. **Rapid relaxation** following a stressful period shifts the body into a state of Low Activation, which signals to the immune system that the stressful period is over.

4. States of Low Activation result in the immune system lowering its defenses, leaving the body less able to fight off illness.

5. The **sudden shift** from High Activation to Low Activation is the essence of the Let-Down Effect.

6. The heaviness, fatigue, and spaciness associated with the Let-Down Effect happens because of lowered blood sugar levels and the body falling

into a state of withdrawal due to lower steroid and endorphin levels. As a result, the body feels depleted.

Chapter 4

IDENTIFYING WHEN THE
THE LET-DOWN EFFECT IS OCCURRING

To fully identify the Let-Down Effect, it is vital that you develop a reference point comprised of physical markers that tell you when your body is healthy. This reference point will make it easy for you to recognize changes in your body that can be an early warning of illness or the start of the Let-Down Effect. Like most medical conditions, early detection is often the best treatment.

I have found in my clinical practice that most people are unaware of what their bodies feel like inside – until they begin to feel sick. Then it becomes easy, for they may notice that they feel run down, achy, exhausted, or notice that their glands are swollen. These sensations become red flags that alert all of us when we are not well.

It can be helpful to think of the body when it is

healthy or normal as being in a state of equilibrium. Internally, this is the sum of many different physiological reactions, which would include heartbeat, blood pressure, body temperature, and hormones. These mechanisms are influenced by our genetic makeup, but also by numerous life experiences.

Understanding what is your normal state of equilibrium becomes important not only for detecting the early signs of illness, but also for ascertaining changes in your activation states. As a starting point for gauging your body's state of health, you can begin by learning how to identify the two main (and most recognizable) types of activation states: Low Activation and High Activation.

By learning how to identify your highs and lows, you will eventually be able to identify your state of equilibrium as somewhere in the middle. More importantly, by learning how to identify when you are in a state of Low or High Activation, you are taking the first step toward blocking the Let-Down Effect.

Let's take a look at these two main states of activation.

We are in a High Activation state when we experience elevated energy. This happens when we engage in certain physical and/or mental activities. Any of the following sensations can be an indication of a High Activation state:

- A highly energized feeling
- Alertness
- Physical tightness in the neck, shoulders, and/or back
- Anxiety, tension, pressure
- Frustration, feeling rushed
- Accelerated heartbeat
- Elevated blood pressure
- Active thoughts; having difficulty turning the mind off
- Fear and a sense of danger
- Anger, hostility, or agitation
- Excitement, happiness, or euphoria

- **Restlessness, hyperactivity**
- **Lightness, tingling**
- **Intensity**
- **Hyped or geared up**

As you can see, a High Activation state can occur when we are happy or when we are stressed. For example, High Activation can occur when we are having a wonderful, exciting, and energized time with friends. Conversely, High Activation is also present if we find ourselves angry or upset often, frustrated in traffic, or racing to meet a deadline.

On the other hand, after completing a stressful project or beginning a vacation, our level of activation generally becomes lower. We begin to relax our guard, both physically and mentally, and our bodies move into a less activated state. In a low activated state, the body feels slower or less energetic, and the mind becomes less active. Instead of feeling a tension or anxiety, we feel calm and still, or a sense of heaviness and sluggishness. The following sensations are indications of Low

Activation:

- Heaviness or sluggishness
- Fatigue
- Slowness or lethargy
- Numbness
- Less active thoughts
- Spaciness
- Relaxation
- Depression
- Calm
- Peacefulness
- Stillness

As you can see, the Low Activation state, like high activation, can be either pleasant or unpleasant.

Of importance is that these activation levels can become like a habit. For example, after many years of experiencing High Activation states as part of accomplishing goals, we may come to associate this state with being productive. In fact, it is not uncommon for some individuals to feel that they cannot be productive without this elevated state.

Eventually, after chronically operating in a High Activation state, it can be difficult to shut off and shift to a lower activation state. Over time, High Activation states begin to occur in situations where they are not needed, such as while watching television or trying to fall asleep.

Many people who suffer from Let-Down-related illnesses seesaw between habitual High Activation states and brief periods of Low Activation and illness.

A Case of Habitual High Activation

Tom, an attorney who came to me for treatment, suffered from frequent upper respiratory infections, such as bronchitis. Being ill cost Tom dearly, for it meant losing work and billable hours. He told me assertively, "Don't tell me that my problem is due to stress, because I never get ill when I am under stress." Tom was right; he did not become sick while under stress- only afterwards.

When I asked him about the conditions that preceded his illness, it became apparent that his symptoms commonly followed the completion of a court case. During the course of a trial, Tom received less sleep, skipped meals, stopped exercising, and ate poorly. During this time, he felt a great pressure to succeed, while the lingering uncertainty as to how the case would be resolved kept his body in an energized state. What Tom described to me was a High Activation state.

When the trial was completed, Tom generally took the rest of that day off, as well as the following day to recover. He described to me how he would sleep late, eat more healthfully, watch TV, and "just veg." Further, Tom described how he felt sluggish, unmotivated, and had a difficult time concentrating. What he was describing was a state of Low Activation, the state in which he typically developed bronchitis. He felt frustrated about getting sick when he was doing all the right things: no stress, relaxation, lots of sleep, and eating all the healthy foods.

Clearly, Tom had made himself more vulnerable to illness due to the stress of the trial. Stress, as well as sleep deprivation, have a harmful effect on the immune system. Yet if Tom's illness were merely related to these compromising factors, Tom would have become sick during the course of the trial. The fact is that Tom consistently became sick *after* the stressful conditions had passed.

The most decisive factor that led to Tom's illness was his **rapid shift** from the High Activation state of the trial to the Low Activation state following the trial. This was a classic example of the Let-Down Effect in action. Once Tom learned how to slow his transition from High Activation to Low Activation, the bronchitis that usually followed his post-trial periods became virtually nonexistent.

Step One: Identifying Activation States in Yourself

As I mentioned earlier, the first step to blocking the Let-Down Effect is to become sensitive to changes in activation states within yourself. The following situations listed in Table 1 are all scenarios in which High Activation can occur.

Please note that you may or may not categorize certain situations in the same way that I have done in this table. That's fine; everyone is different. You may observe that the degree of activation is contingent on the specific situation. For example, in some situations you may feel a very high level of activation, while in others you may feel only a moderate level of activation. You may even categorize one or more of the items on this list as a Low Activation situation rather than a High Activation situation.

As you go through the list of situations, try to imagine yourself in each one. Pay particular attention to the sensations that your body is feeling. Use the list of High Activation sensations (page 30) as your guide. Remember that activation states are expressed in terms of sensation. The more aware you become of how you feel physically, the more alert you become to those sensations that are aligned with health, and those that are aligned with illness.

See if you feel levels of High Activation in all of these situations? Or do you instead identify High Activation in only several of the situations?

You may also find that not all of the situations are ultimately subject to the Let-Down Effect in your own life. For example, you may observe that you are more likely to become ill after having a conflict with a friend, but remain healthy after sharing happy times with friends. Or, you may notice that the reverse is true. You may also come to learn that there are a number of other situations that are precursors to the Let-Down Effect. See Table 1.

Table 1
HIGH ACTIVATION SITUATIONS

1.   You are late for an appointment, and trapped in traffic.
2.   You are feeling great pressure to complete a project or assignment.
3.   You are rushing to get ready for work or attempting to get the kids off to school on time.
4.   You are having a conflict with a friend or coworker.
5.   You feel frustrated about not being able to accomplish a task or goal.
6.   You are having a wonderful or mentally and emotionally stimulating time with your friends or partner.
7.   You are involved in an exercise activity, such as jogging, or a competitive sport, such as tennis or basketball.
8.   You are successfully completing your work and handling multiple tasks at one time.
9.   Your body feels healthy and energetic.
10. You are successful in completing an important goal.
11. You are giving an important presentation.

The following situations in Table 2 are all scenarios in which Low Activation can occur. Again, you may or may not categorize all of these situations as I have done. For you, some of these situations may be more apt to create Low Activation than others. A couple may even create High Activation. Again, look at each situation on the list and try to imagine experiencing it. Pay attention to the sensations in your body as you picture each situation. Use the list of Low Activation sensations (p 32) as your guide.

See if you notice Low Activation levels in all of the situations, or only in a few of them. Or do you notice different degrees of Low Activation based on the particular situation? For example, would you experience a feeling of mild sluggishness after going home on Friday, but an extreme heaviness on the last day of your vacation.

Table 2
LOW ACTIVATION SITUATIONS

1. You have just awakened in the morning.
2. You have just completed lunch or dinner.
3. You have been under stress at work and have completed a project, deadline, or meeting several hours earlier.
4. You have finished your work day, and you are leaving the office.
5. You are preparing to go to sleep
6. You have been on vacation for several days.
7. You have finished a strenuous workout or exercise routine several hours earlier.
8. You have completed your work week and are beginning the weekend.
9. It is several hours later or the next day after having great time with friends or at a social event.
10. It is the last day of your vacation, and you are returning home.
11. You are on the verge of being sick.
12. You are currently feeling ill.
13. Several hours earlier you resolved a conflict that had been a source of tension for you.
14. You're spending a quiet evening watching a movie with a good friend or your partner.

Working with these tables should help you to key into the specific physical sensations you experience while in these different situations. Once you pinpoint the sensations connected with each situation, the tables will show whether these sensations indicate a state of Low or High Activation. Now you know which situations in your life put you in a state of High Activation, and which put you in a state of Low Activation

Now that you have become acquainted with High and Low Activation states, it is now important to determine when you are most apt to become ill due to the **rapid** fluctuation of activation levels.

There are three main reaction styles that lead to activation-related illnesses. Answer the questions in Table 3 on page 43.

For most individuals, the Let-Down Effect begins within a day or two after shifting from High to Low Activation. The Let-Down Effect may last as little as one day or a matter of weeks. In some cases, the Let-Down Effect can stretch over a longer period of time, even extending to a number of months. This can be the case when individuals have been strenuously working for a prolonged stretch (months or a year) on a specific project or goal. Once completed, the individual remains in a lethargic, unmotivated, or even unfocused state for a matter of months. This type of Let-Down Effect can become the genesis of Chronic Fatigue Syndrome, Fibromyalgia, or chronic sinusitis.

If you found that you are an Immediate or Delayed Reactor, then the cause of your illness is, in one respect, the opposite of the Let-Down Effect. Let-Down Reactors are vulnerable to shifts from High to Low Activation, while Immediate and Delayed Reactors get sick after shifting from Low to High Activation. **All three types of individuals, however, have one thing in common: Their symptoms result from a rapid shifting of activation levels.**

Preventing the Let-Down Reaction, therefore, requires lengthening the transition from High to Low Activation. In a similar manner, preventing Immediate and Delayed Reactions requires lengthening the

Table 3
THE THREE REACTOR TYPES

1. Do you feel ill or experience symptoms after you have shifted from a state of High Activation to a state of Low Activation?
   If so, you are a true **Let-Down Effect Reactor**
   If we think of stress as a battle, then the Let-Down Reactor becomes sick after the battle is over or is won.

2. Do you become ill or experience symptoms in the early stages of High Activation, but only after having come out of a prolonged period of Low Activation?
   If so, you are a **Delayed Reactor.**
   The Delayed Reactor becomes sick either in anticipation of the battle or in the early stages of battle —and always after a prolonged period of peace time.
   For example, Delayed Reactors would not become ill while on vacation. Instead, they would become ill either on the day they return home from vacation or on the first day back at work.

3. Do you become ill or experience symptoms during a state of High Activation?
   If so, you are an **Immediate Reactor**
   The Immediate Reactor becomes sick in the heat of battle.
   Unlike the Delayed Reactor, Immediate Reactors do require a prolonged down time to precede the onset of their illness.

transition from Low to High Activation. You will learn to change the transition pace between activation levels in Chapters 6 and 7.

Did you find yourself answering yes to two or all three questions? If so, this would alert you to the possibility that there are several different causes of your activation-related illnesses, with each requiring a slightly different solution.

In the next chapter, you will learn to more precisely identify the different levels of "speed" within each of the two main activation states.

Chapter 4 Summary:

1. High Activation is often associated with being alert, energetic, and engaging in vigorous physical and/or mental activity.

2. High Activation can occur in both positive and negative situations.

3. Low Activation can also occur in both positive and negative situations. Its positive attributes include calm, relaxation, and stillness. Its negative attributes can include fatigue, sluggishness, and depression.

4. There are three main styles that lead to activation-related illnesses.

    a. **Let-Down Reactor** (illness occurs as a result of a sudden shift from High Activation to Low Activation). Let-Down Reactors become sick after the battle is won.

    b. **Delayed Reactor** (illness occurs in the early stages of High Activation, but only after coming out of a prolonged period of Low Activation). Delayed Reactors become sick either in anticipation of the battle or in the early stages of the battle.

c.   **Immediate Reactor** (illness occurs after a rapid shift to High Activation from only a brief, slightly lower state of activation). Immediate Reactors become sick in the heat of battle.

Chapter 5

YOUR ACTIVATION SPEED

In the previous chapter, you began the process of identifying Low and High Activation levels within yourself, as well as their relationship to different situations that you encounter. You may have noticed that not all situations are alike in their effect on activation levels. For example, you may have observed that certain situations provoke very high levels of activation, while others elicit only moderate levels of activation. For our purposes, it is useful to think about activation levels in terms of miles per hour. The higher speeds represent greater levels of activation, while the lower speeds represent lesser levels of activation.

The best way to identify at which speed your body is "traveling" is to observe the physical sensations that accompany a particular speed of activation. Let's say that 100 miles per hour (MPH) represents the highest level of activation. Let's also suppose that in your case, one of the situations in which you would experience a 100 MPH activation level is when you become embroiled in an intense argument. The physical sensations that accompany this highest level of activation may be heart palpitations, shortness of breath, and dizziness.

The following table (Table 4) details a range of activation speeds next to various situations and the physical sensations that may accompany them. As in the previous tables in this book, please note that this table is only a guide. You may or may not categorize a particular scenario at the same speed that I have. What is most important is that you begin to pinpoint how your body and your mind speed up or slow down in response to the various situations in your own life.

Table 4

SPEED TABLE

	Sensation	Physical Sensation
100 MPH	Intense Anger, Trauma	Rapid Heart Beat, Dizzy, Shallow Breath
90 MPH	Project Deadline, Sports Competition	Pressure, Anxiety Tingling
80 MPH	Late to Work, Stuck in Traffic	Tense, Tightness, Hyper
75 MPH	Meeting an Exciting New Person	Excited, Energized, Restless
70 MPH	Presentation	Focused, Feeling "on" Scared, Nervous
65 MPH	Exercise-Jogging, Swimming, Sports	Energy, Alert, Absorbed
60 MPH	Running Errands, Work Tasks	Alert, Active Mind

Table 4
(Continued)

	Situation	Physical Sensation
50 MPH	Pleasurable Evening with Friends	Lightness, Warmth,
40 MPH	No Pressing Demands	Calm, Quietness
30 MPH	Vacation	Slow, Peaceful, Still, Heavy
10 MPH	Pre-Illness, Sad	Fatigue, Lethargic
5 MPH	Illness	Numb, Sluggish

You can see from the chart that both positive and negative events can create High Activation. Typically, however, negative events or circumstances create the highest levels of activation and are ultimately more physically harmful than positive events. On the other hand, we almost always associate Low Activation with very pleasurable activities. For most of us, feeling deeply relaxed, having our minds and bodies quiet, and feeling no pressure can be a wonderful respite from our normal routine. However, depression and sluggishness can also be Low Activation experiences. Therefore, we can say that in general, the extremes of High and Low Activation are what pose a potential problem.

Nevertheless, if you are a Let-Down Reactor, what is most important to remember is this: **It is the *rapid transition* from High Activation to Low Activation that is most responsible for the Let-Down Effect.** An example of a rapid transition would be going from a speed of 70 or 80 MPH to a speed of 20 to 30 MPH in the course of hours or one day. Ideally, to avoid the Let-Down Effect it is necessary to taper down our speed. The first day, we would brake from 70 to 50 MPH. On the next day, we would slow from 50 MPH to 30 MPH.

In the next chapter, you will begin learning the tools you need to slow your activation in a gradual way. In so doing, you will avoid the Let-Down Effect. Later in the book you will also learn how to adjust your activation if you are a Delayed Reactor or an Immediate Reactor.

Chapter 5 Summary:

1. We can think of activation levels in the body in terms of miles per hour. The higher the speed of our mental or physical activity, the higher our activation level. The lower the speed of our activity, the lower the activation level.

2. Both pleasurable and negative activities are responsible for different activation speeds.

3. To avoid the Let-Down Effect, it is important that we learn how to reduce our activation speed in a gradual manner.

Chapter 6

SOMAFOCUS [1]

In the last two chapters, you learned to identify the various sensations associated with your High and Low Activation states. This is the first step to learning how to alter your activation states. With a tool that I call **Somafocus**, you will learn how to actively modify physical sensations in your body. Somafocus will give you the ability to use these physical sensations to manipulate your activation states.

Remember that we are most vulnerable to the Let-Down Effect when we abruptly shift from a state of High Activation to a state of Low Activation. Therefore, my goal is to help you make this transition much more gradual. **By modifying your physical sensations through Somafocus, you can slow the transition from High Activation to Low Activation.**

Somafocus delays the onset of Low Activation

1- Somafocus is a Registered Trademark, 2001

54

by moderately elevating activation levels. A number of studies have found that moderate elevations in activation result in an enhanced immune response, such as increases in Natural Killer Cells. **Therefore, Somafocus not only blocks the Let-Down Effect, but it also has the ability to enhance our immune response.**

For many years the prevailing belief was that when we mentally changed the physical sensations in our bodies, we were merely imagining them to be different. It was believed that despite our perceptions, nothing had chemically or physiologically changed in our bodies. This assumption sprang from the belief that the mind and body were separate, which implied that our thoughts had no effect on our bodies, and vice versa.

Over the last 10 years, much research has shown that, in fact, what we think or feel does indeed have an effect on our bodies' chemistry. These effects range from changing the way our brain cells function to enhancing or suppressing our immune system.

Many readers are likely familiar with the technique of visualization and how it has been used to affect the health of the body. In my clinical work, I have learned that Somafocus is a much more powerful tool for creating physical change than relying on visualization alone. Although vision is our dominant sense, many people who use visualization often feel like they are observers, rather than active participants. One reason for this is that many of us have become conditioned to be visually passive, due to habitual watching of films or television. By enabling us to be more actively present and involved, Somafocus creates much more profound physical effects on our bodies than visualization alone. It not only alters the physical sensations in the body, but it can also change the body's chemistry.

What is also interesting about Somafocus is that we can use this tool to focus on specific parts of the body. In our study at UCLA, we found that the participants who used a Somafocus technique were able to affect their Helper T cell (an immune cell) count in the area of the skin in which they directed the technique. Further, these same subjects were able to speed the healing time in their forearms after receiving a tetanus injection just under their skin (similar to a TB shot). The tetanus injection had caused an inflammation in their forearms, and they used Somafocus to heal their forearms of the inflammation.

Several other studies have also found that it is possible to direct the mind to specific parts of the body to induce healing. In one particular study, one group of subjects received hypnosis to rid the body of warts. The second group received a topical solution to remove the warts. A control group received no treatment. The group that received the hypnosis had significantly superior success in eradicating their warts than the other two groups. Related studies have found that the mind can effectively alter blood flow and skin temperature in one hand while not affecting the other hand.

Somafocus gives us the ability to either target our interventions to specific parts of our bodies or to apply it in a larger way to change activation states in our bodies. See Table 5 for a partial list of some of the mind's documented effects on the body or health.

Table 5

THE DIFFERENT WAYS THE MIND AFFECTS THE BODY

1. The immune system
2. Circulation of the blood
3. Inflammation
4. Colonic motility or movement of the intestines
5. The vascular flow in the brain
6. The experience of pain
7. Post surgical recovery
   - Rapid healing of the body
   - Less pain medications

Table 5
(Continued)
8. EEG or brain waves
9. The warmth or coolness of our limbs
10. Eczema and other skin reactions
11. Gastric secretions (stomach acid)
12. Heartbeat/pulse
13. Blood pressure
14. Hormones
15. Cholesterol
16. Blood sugar levels
17. Menstrual cycle

The Role of Confidence and Practice

In order to use Somafocus effectively to create positive health benefits, it is first necessary to develop your skills and **confidence** in manipulating your physiology. The importance of confidence cannot be understated.

Many of us have come to accept a certain set of limited beliefs about our ability to control the body or our health. We were not raised with the idea that the mind can influence the body. Due to this upbringing, we may approach these ideas with a certain level of skepticism. Or, we may feel that it is intuitively possible, but we lack the **confidence** in our ability to make it work. Since these belief systems are fairly common due to our upbringing, you are not alone if you should feel skeptical or a lack of confidence.

Through the years, there have been so many things that mankind felt were impossible, whether it was flying, curing certain illnesses, or traveling to the moon. There were always people who said it could not be done. What you are about to learn represents another major milestone in affecting your health.

Unlike many important moments in history that have challenged people's belief systems, with Somafocus we need not operate on faith alone until science proves otherwise. The fact is there is a great body of scientific research that supports the mind-body connection. Equally important is that most of this research has been conducted on individuals who have been raised with the same limiting beliefs as the rest of us, rather than on individuals who have special training in this area.

Nearly everyone is capable of learning how to affect his or her health through the mind-body connection. Challenge yourself to approach the Somafocus exercises with an open mind. Skepticism can be healthy, but it can also serve to protect us from having to change our beliefs. Nonetheless, if you think of yourself as a die-hard skeptic, consider the following situation. Have you ever found yourself yawning and feeling tired as a result of being in the company of another person who consistently yawns? This effect can occur even if we were not tired before being around this person. This particular example of the power of suggestion is so common that most of us do not give it a second thought. However, it clearly demonstrates that the mind can have an influence on the body – whether we are aware of it or not.

When you start exploring the Somafocus techniques, view them as you would any other new task; know that with practice you will continue to improve. View your success in terms of increments, rather than all or nothing. As you succeed, let your confidence develop in increments as well.

If you succeed at first, but then do not succeed with another technique, do not assume that your first success was a fluke. You will find that there will be certain techniques that you will find easy to do, while others you may find more difficult. This is true for everyone. **It is <u>not</u> important to be successful in all of the techniques. Rather, it is important to learn which Somafocus techniques are best at creating moderately higher activation levels within you.**

The following Somafocus techniques mark the beginning of your exciting journey into learning what you can do to regain control over your body and health. Some of the techniques may appear simple to you. It would be natural to wonder how something so simple could actually have any true physical effect. Nevertheless, by creating health enhancing, physical sensations in your body, these techniques have been found to alter your physiology and body chemistry, and thereby, your **activation level**. As you learn to alter your activation level, you then have the tools to positively affect your health.

Some of these exercises you may have partially experienced before. What is unique about these exercises is that they are paired with an emphasis on creating specific health enhancing, physical sensations in your body, which will become augmented with practice.

Table 6 lists the different sensations that you may experience while altering your mind and body activation levels. You may experience one or all of these sensations during these Somafocus techniques. Use this table as a reference point to assess your success in modifying your activation level through the following series of Somafocus exercises.

Some of the following techniques may be activities or exercises that you are already familiar with

Table 6

ACTIVATION INDICATORS

1. **Alertness**
2. **Lightness**
3. **Tingling**
4. **Energy**
5. **Restless**
6. **Mind feels more active**
7. **Some level of tension in the body**
8. **Vibration or pulsation**

doing. In these situations, you are using these familiar activities to create a physical sensation in your body that elevates your activation level. Once this sensation is created, you will then ultimately use this sensation to block the Let Down Effect. With practice you may find that you can trigger this sensation through Somafocus, merely by concentrating on this sensation.

Please note that **it is not essential to create profound alterations in activation levels with Somafocus in order to have a healing effect. Instead,** only moderate elevations of activation levels are ultimately necessary to block the Let-Down Effect. Therefore, as you perform the Somafocus exercises, feel pleased with even mild alterations of activation.

Technique 1:   Conjuring up the Past

The technique of Conjuring up the Past is a powerful means of harnessing our natural mind-body capability. In this technique, you will treat your body to the kinds of thoughts and feelings that alter your biochemistry in a positive manner. By recalling past events that the mind associates with a healthy level of activation, you can also summon the healing properties of these events while moderately elevating the body's activation level. This technique is akin to swallowing a healing medicine or vitamin.

Begin by sitting comfortably in a chair. Allow your mind to select a recent or past experience that you associate with a feeling of excitement, energy, or positive feelings. For example, recall a time when you experienced the thrill of having completed an important personal or work goal. You can also think of a vacation or a fun place that you visited that was associated with joy or positive feelings. Finally, you can remember the excitement you felt with someone you met recently.

As you recall this experience, see if you can recapture the feeling of energy or excitement in the body. Think of the thoughts you were having at the time, how your body was feeling, or what you or other people were saying at the time. Pretend as if you are actually re-experiencing this event in all of its detail. Experience the external sounds, the weather, and physical sensations in your body. After a few moments, see if your body or mind has started to feel differently. For example, does your head and/or chest feel lighter? Has your mood changed as well? Do other parts of your body feel different, such as your fingers, feet, or shoulders? Are they feeling warm, tingly, or light? Do you feel more activated or energized?

Once you become aware of any of these activation indicators, take a moment to close your eyes and focus on them. For example, if you feel a slight warmth in your body, then focus your attention on the part of the body that feels this sensation. Attempt to intensify the warmth by focusing on it. In amplifying the warmth, you are, in fact, raising your activation level further. See how warm you can make it.

Technique 2:   **Lightness and Floating Exercise**

Sit comfortably on a chair with armrests, with your feet on the ground. Place your hands and arms on the armrests, with your palms facing down. Next, with your elbows remaining on the armrest, *very slowly* begin to move both of your forearms upward, while letting your wrists hang loosely downward. You can even imagine that your arms are moving up almost by themselves. Or, you can pretend that your wrists are being pulled by helium inflated balloons. Allow your arms to move up to a 45-degree angle from the armrest.

1.   As your arms move upward, do you feel a lifting sensation? Do your arms feel as if they are moving almost on their own?

2.   Do you feel a lightness in your arms or hands?

3.   Which arm feels lighter than the other?

4.   After leaving your arms in this position for a few minutes, have you noticed that you have become either less aware or unaware of your arms and their position?

Part 2:

With your arms continuing to remain elevated, close your eyes and direct your attention to the middle of your forehead. While inhaling slowly through your nose, imagine a light or floating feeling developing in your forehead.   Sometimes it can be helpful to imagine yourself floating on a raft or being lifted up by a cloud. Be careful not to rely solely on visualization for this exercise, however. It is easy to fall into the trap of merely visualizing rather than trying to create the physical feeling of floating.

1.   Do you feel a lightness or floating sensation?

2.   Does this sensation become stronger the longer you focus on it?

3.   Do you feel it only in one part of your head, or all over?

4.   If you are having difficulties creating the floating or lightness, then focus instead on the top of your head, halfway between the crown of your head and your forehead. See if you can create a sensation of lightness and floating in this area.

Technique 3: Mental Problem Solving

Another means of raising activation levels is to perform mental problem solving exercises. Several studies have found that mental problem solving conducted under time constraints has led to an activation of the immune response. Experiment with the following problem solving tasks

1. Quickly calculate in your head a series of math questions. Based on your ability, determine how complex the problems need to be in order to create vigorous mental activity. For example, some of you may find that calculating 12 times 36 creates an adequate challenge. Others may require more complex problems, such as 122 times 366.

   Here are some examples of more math problems to solve:

   A. How many American dollars is 1,256 English pounds?

   B. How many cents or dollars do you earn in a second?

   C. How many heartbeats would you have over 75 years?

2. Quickly do some word problems, such as

70

solving a couple of entries in a challenging crossword puzzle, or writing down a number of random letters and trying to form as many different words from them as you can. Play a game of Concentration with cards or numbers.

3. Create analogies in your mind, making them increasingly more complex, such as:

A. The Earth is to the sun, as the solar system is the galaxy

B. Red is to blue (both primary colors), as 11 is to 13 (both prime numbers).

It is not critical that you solve all the problems correctly, but rather that you create enough energy in your body and mind to elevate your activation level. Therefore, continue solving problems until you feel your mind and/or body increasing your level of activation. For most individuals this would require about five to ten minutes of problem solving, if you are

71

pushing yourself to rapidly solve the problems.

By the way, group games such as Rummycub can be a fun and healthy way to raise your activation levels for longer stretches of time, such as while on vacation or during the weekends. Not only do these word games stimulate the mind and raise the level of humor, but they will also be working to elevate your activation levels during your extended periods of down time.

As you work on the mental problem solving exercises, compare your responses to those listed on the Activation Indicators (Table 6, page 64). Which indicator(s) are you feeling? Select one that you will focus your attention on next. For example, if the problem solving led you to feel a tingly or electricity like feeling in your neck and head, then close your eyes and focus on this sensation. See if you can intensify this feeling. Intensifying the feeling is a way to raise your activation level further.

Technique 4: The Vibration Technique

The goal of this technique is to create a vibration, warmth, or lightness in your shoulders, neck, and/or head. This technique can rapidly infuse the body with these positive and activating sensations.

Begin by standing and facing a window. Close your eyes, and allow your mouth and jaw to drop open. With your arms straight, elbows slightly bent, and holding them just below shoulder level, reach out and lightly lay the open palms of your hands on the window. Then take two steps back from the window while maintaining the position of your arms and open palms. Begin to rhythmically, repeatedly, and lightly move your arms (only bending the elbow slightly from its position) and hands, backwards and forwards, as if you were pushing air toward the window.

Another example of this motion would be the movement you make when you are closing a drawer with two hands or giving someone a gentle push on their back. Continue this motion for approximately

10 to15 seconds.

Next, begin to speed up the pace of the vibration of your hands and arms, while still only bending your arms and elbows slightly. Continue for another 10 to 15 seconds. Next, pick the pace up to a much faster level. As you do this, you will feel your head, shoulders, neck, and your upper torso beginning to gently vibrate and shake . Imagine that your entire body is becoming synchronized to the rhythm of your arms and hands.

After 15 seconds place your arms and hands at your side, and let the entire body become still and close your eyes. Focus on the sensations in your head, shoulders, and chest. See if you can feel a vibration, warmth, or tingling. Once you feel any of these sensations, then focus your attention on them and see if you can further intensify these sensations. Boosting the strength of these sensations is a way of raising your activation level.

Technique 5: Physical Activity

Many studies have found that even mild exercise can lead to immune enhancement. That is why this technique uses brief but rapid walking to create activation. This can be accomplished in the following ways:

1.	Take a brief walk outside for five minutes. If possible, exaggerate your arm and hand movements as you walk.

2.	If you are unable to go outside, walk through your house in a rapid manner. If possible, exaggerate your arm and hand movements as you walk.

3.	If you are at work, go up and down several flights of stairs. Or, rapidly walk a brief distance from your work station to another location and repeat several times.

4.	If you are comfortable with jogging, take a moderate jog for 5 to 10 minutes.

Remember that in this technique, your goal is

not to have a complete workout. Instead, your goal is to bring your activation level to a higher level. As in the previous techniques, compare what you are feeling with the activation indicators in Table 6 (page 64). Identify which activation indicator(s) is strongest. Close your eyes and focus on this sensation. See if it begins to amplify. If so, you are then able to raise your activation level to an even higher level.

With experience and confidence, you may find that you can raise your activation level merely by closing your eyes and focusing on specific sensations in your body. This is the hallmark advantage of Somafocus. By merely focusing on these sensations and raising our activation levels, we are able to alter our body chemistry and boost our immune response. and block the Let-Down Effect.

Chapter 6 Summary:

1. Somafocus delays the onset of Low Activation by moderately elevating activation levels.

2. Somafocus not only blocks the Let-Down Effect, but it also has the ability to enhance our immune response.

3. The mind is capable of affecting the body in multiple ways, from the immune system and blood circulation, to inflammation and the experience of pain.

4. There are five Somafocus Activation Techniques:

    a.   Conjuring up the Past

    b.   Lightness and Floating

    c.   Mental Problem Solving

    d.   The Vibration Technique

    e.   Physical Activity

Chapter 7

STOPPING THE LET-DOWN EFFECT
AND BLOCKING THE DELAYED
REACTOR EFFECT

In the previous chapter, you learned to use Somafocus techniques to create sensations such as energy, warmth, lightness, and floating in different parts of your body. By creating these different sensations, you have actually learned to manipulate your body's physiology and chemistry, and thereby, your activation levels.

In this chapter, I will explain how to use Somafocus to block the Let-Down Effect and the Delayed-Reactor Effect. First, let's start with the Let-Down Effect.

Counteracting the Let-Down Effect

Remember, the Let-Down Effect is a result of a **rapid** transition from a High Activation state to a Low

Activation state. The key to halting the Let-Down Effect is to make the transition between the two activation states more gradual. **Using Somafocus techniques will enable you to delay the onset of Low Activation.**

To begin this process, refer back to Chapter Three, Table 1, which lists a number of potential High Activation situations (page 38). Select the one(s) that you believe are a precursor to the Let-Down Effect. In other words, pinpoint the situations that have immediately preceded your past illnesses.

Let's say that you generally become ill several hours or a day following a stressful project. The next time you find yourself involved in a similar project, do the following as a preventive measure and/or at the first sign of symptoms:

1.   As soon as it is reasonably possible after finishing the project, begin using the Somafocus technique you were most successful with in the previous chapter

(Chapter 6). If, for example, you were most successful with the Somafocus technique of Conjuring up the Past, then use this technique first. Spend three to five minutes doing it.

2. Use this Somafocus technique a total of two to three times that day and two to three times the next day.

3. If for example, you have been traveling at 80 MPH while working on the project, then remind yourself that you are only going to slow to 60 MPH during the course of the day. If you are not sure what it should feel like to be at 80 or 60 MPH, refer to the Speed Table (page 49) in Chapter 5. Look at the list of the physical sensations that you may experience at the various speeds.

4. At any sign of Low Activation (refer to Table 2, page 40), repeat the Somafocus

technique as soon as possible to counter the Low Activation sensations, such as sluggishness or slowness. If you are experiencing these sensations, then there is a good chance that you have dropped from 80 MPH to 30 MPH, rather than to 60 MPH. Those Low Activation sensations are a signal that your Activation Speed has slowed too quickly.

5. If you are unable to counter the Low Activation sensations in Step 4, then try one of the other Somafocus techniques that you were successful with in the previous chapter. Continue to remind yourself that you are to remain at 60 MPH and that you are not going to slow down too **quickly**.

6. If by the end of the day or the next day you have not experienced any Low

Activation symptoms, allow yourself to downshift your Activation Speed to 40 MPH. However, continue using the Somafocus technique two to three times during the day.

7. If you are on vacation, wait until the second or third day before allowing yourself to slow your Activation level to 30 MPH.

If you have managed to avoid becoming sick or experiencing any symptoms, congratulations. You have succeeded in beating the Let-Down Effect. If you still become sick after going through the above steps, then it is necessary to do the following:

1. Try one of the other Somafocus techniques, such as the Floating Technique. Or, use the original Somafocus technique more frequently, such as four to five times a day.

2.   Lower your Activation MPH at a slower pace. Instead of dropping from 80 to 60 MPH on the first day, reduce your speed to 70 MPH. On the following day, you can slow down to 50 MPH.

Blocking the Delayed-Reactor Effect

Remember, you are a Delayed Reactor if you become sick after returning from a vacation or a break. People who are Delayed Reactors often complain that they become sick on Sunday nights, the day they are returning from vacation, or on their first day back at work after their vacation.

Delayed Reactions are caused by a rapid transition from a Low Activation state to a High Activation state. Although this is the **opposite** of the Let-Down Effect, Delayed Reactors can use the same Somafocus techniques that Let-Down Reactors use. Your goal if you are a Delayed Reactor, however, is to **slow** the transition from Low Activation to High

Activation. Somafocus achieves this by gradually raising your Activation Level. In so doing, when you return to work you are not suddenly shifting from 30 MPH to 80 MPH, which is harmful for the Delayed Reactor.

Let's say you have noticed that you are most vulnerable to becoming sick the day prior to returning to work. If so, on the day before you return to work, do the following to innoculate yourself.

1.   If you have been cruising at 30 MPH over the last few days, then remind yourself that you are now going to accelerate your pace to 50 MPH.

2   Start using the Somafocus technique (whichever one is easiest for you to do) to begin **raising** your Activation level within the target Activation Speed of 50 MPH. Repeat this Somafocus technique two to three times during the day to maintain this target speed.

3.   The following day, use the Somafocus technique two to three times a day to raise your Activation

Speed to 60 MPH.

If you still get sick after going through the above steps, do the following:

1. Try one of the other Somafocus techniques, such as the Floating Technique. Or, use the original Somafocus technique more frequently, such as four to five times a day.

2. Raise your Activation MPH at a slower pace. Instead of elevating your speed from 30 to 50 MPH on the first day, raise your speed to 40 MPH. On the following day, you can speed up to 60 MPH. If you find that your are raising your activation too quickly, you will want to use one of the Limiting Activation Techniques discussed in Chapter 10.

Practice Patience

It is important when learning to block the Let-Down and Delayed-Reactor Effects that you expect there to be a learning curve. Be realistic about your expectations. Practice and experience are critical. For example, if you frequently develop colds due to the Let-Down Effect, then initially you may be able to prevent this from happening 45% of the time. With practice, you may able to prevent your colds 70 to 90% of the time. Or, you may find that with some conditions you can stop the Let-Down Effect with nearly a 100% track record, while with other conditions, your percentage might remain at 60%. With practice, you have the best chance of increasing these percentages.

You may find yourself becoming easily discouraged on those occasions when your use of Somafocus fails to block the Let-Down Effect. You may feel this way even if you have succeeded previously in blocking the Let-Down Effect. It seems to be a human tendency to attribute much more significance to our failures than to our successes. However, if you succeeded the first time you used Somafocus but did not succeed the second time, you are still one for two.

Stated differently, your success rate is 50%, which means that you are cutting in half your chances of becoming sick. In medicine, interventions that reduce illness by 30 to 50% are typically considered to be very successful.

Allow each success to build your beliefs and confidence in using your mind to make a difference in your body. Remember that your level of **confidence** plays a major role in boosting the effectiveness of Somafocus. Research has extensively evaluated and proven the role that confidence and positive thinking play in our health. Therefore, the more you can believe in your ability to make a difference, the greater chance you have of positively affecting your health. Keep in mind that positive belief systems and confidence literally create biochemical reactions in your body, reactions that can bolster your chances of positively affecting your health.

Chapter 7 Summary:

1. Somafocus is a tool for dealing with the Let-Down Effect, the Delayed-Reactor Effect, and the first onset of physical symptoms.

2. In order to block the Let-Down Effect, Somafocus **slows** the transition from High Activation to Low Activation.

3. In order to block the Delayed-Reactor Effect, Somafocus **slows** the transition from Low Activation to High Activation.

4. Be realistic in your expectations. Expect that practice will improve your ability. Confidence plays a major role in boosting the effectiveness of Somafocus.

Chapter 8

CONDITIONING AND SOMAFOCUS

I had not eaten all day, and I was eagerly looking forward to dinner at Ricardo's, which served the best chili in Texas. I could already taste the spices as I prepared for my first spoonful. In no time, the chili was gone, leaving me with that nice satisfied feeling that we get after an appetizing meal.

Later that night, I was left with a different feeling – and it was a bad one. Waves of nausea ripped through my body, while a throbbing headache seized control of my head. Soon I was feverish and my body was aching. Somehow I had managed to come down with the flu.

Once I recovered from the short bout with the flu, the prospect of ever having chili again was quite remote. The mere thought of chili, even months later, was enough to induce nausea in me. My bout with the flu had **conditioned** me to associate nausea with chili.

Conditioning, which is often overlooked in health care, plays a major role in our health. In fact, research studies have determined that even our immune system is subject to conditioning. In these studies, rats were given saccharine-flavored water with an immune-enhancing ingredient. After a period of time, the researchers took the immune-enhancing ingredient out of the saccharin-flavored water. However, due to conditioning, just the saccharine taste alone was enough to boost the rats' immune systems.

The implications of these studies are immense. The results suggest that our feelings, behavior, and our thoughts are ultimately capable of becoming conditioned to either healthy or unhealthy physical states. These same feelings, thoughts, and behaviors then take on the power to make us healthy or make us sick.

This type of health conditioning is pervasive in our everyday lives. Once we forge this conditioning bond, we become overly sensitive to the preceding events (**antecedents**) that led to particular health outcomes. This means that an event similar to the antecedent can make us sick even if the event is inherently harmless. For example, if we once developed a cold after being exposed to a draft, we can in the future come down with a cold the next time we encounter a draft. This cold can occur even if the draft we encounter is benign. Or, if we eat the same type of food that once made us sick, we can get sick again – even if the food is devoid of any harmful bacteria.

In either example, our **association** of a particular type of event with illness, in and of itself, has the power to create illness. This type of conditioning is caused by immunological memory, which means that the immune system becomes accustomed to reacting in a certain manner to certain factors.

Conditioning has strong implications for those of us who are vulnerable to the Let-Down Effect as well as for those who are Delayed Reactors or Immediate Reactors. For example, if a Let-Down Reactor has become conditioned to developing illness on vacations or after completing major tasks, then these same events become capable of suppressing his immune system in the future – whether or not there is any stress or other negative factor attached to the future event.

Reconditioning Ourselves With Somafocus

By using Somafocus techniques, we condition our health in a productive manner and reverse negative conditioning patterns. When we apply the Somafocus technique during situations that we associate with sickness, we can block biochemical events in our bodies that lead to physical symptoms. Through a process of what I call **Sensory Competition**, Somafocus creates positive sensations that successfully compete with the negative sensations that usually lead to illness or symptoms. In this manner, the antecedents previously associated with illness begin to lose their negative power over our health. In some cases, Somafocus will have such a positive effect on these antecedents, that they will even begin to have an immune enhancement effect.

A good example of using Somafocus in this manner is of a patient who came to see me because she was suffering from migraine headaches. I learned through a series of questions that Jeannie had become conditioned to developing migraines whenever she was in an environment with fluorescent lights. After years of having this conditioned response, even the anticipation of being in a room with fluorescent lights was sufficient to create a headache. Jeannie's body had simply fallen into the habit of developing headaches at these times.

To counter her headache condition, Jeannie began using the Floating Technique (see Chapter 6) whenever she was exposed to fluorescent lights. As soon as she felt her head and neck began to tighten (which signaled the beginning of her headache), she began creating a floaty and light sensation in her head. The floaty and light sensation created by this technique

competed with the sensations of tightness in her head. The presence of the light and floaty feelings in her head stopped the tightness and kept her from developing a headache. The positive floating sensation altered the biochemistry within her head so that the internal conditions that typically caused a headache were no longer present.

As Jeannie continued to apply this technique in these situations, she began to **recondition** her body to react differently to situations in which there were fluorescent lights. Stated in a different way, Jeannie was able to break the body's habit of developing headaches when exposed to fluorescent lights.

The process of conditioning has other implications as well. In the same manner that we can develop negative symptoms due to conditioning, it is also possible for certain situations or experiences to lead to positive health. Try to identify the situations in your life that you associate with good health. For example, I have always found the ocean and mountain streams to be a trigger for health in my life. By using Somafocus to conjure up (Chapter 6) the sensations I feel in these nature settings, I can enhance my immune response in the times when I need it or even in situations that might be aversive to my health.

Chapter 8 Summary:

1. Our immune system can become conditioned to thoughts, feelings, and behavior, which then have the power to make us healthy or make us sick.

2. Somafocus makes it possible to recondition our body to respond in a healthy manner to certain situations that may have made us sick in the past.

3. Through Sensory Competition, Somafocus creates positive sensations in the body that successfully compete with the negative sensations that would typically lead to illness.

4. We can also positively condition our immune system by conjuring up past situations that we associate with good health.

Chapter 9

SENSITIZATION- THE LONG TERM
RESULT OF THE LET- DOWN EFFECT

For most of us, the Let-Down Effect initially follows periods of intense stress or high levels of activation. We have discussed how a High Activation speed of 80 MPH that immediately drops to a Low Activation speed of 40 MPH can lead to the Let-Down Effect. Unfortunately, as we continue to experience the sudden shifts from High Activation to Low Activation throughout our lives, our bodies become increasingly sensitive to these shifts. Our growing sensitivity can eventually lead to situations in which the Let-Down Effect occurs even when there are less abrupt shifts between the Activation states.

With this greater sensitivity, Low Activation states of 40 MPH that follow a moderate High Activation state of 60 or even 50 MPH can trigger the Let-Down Effect. Where previously a significant amount of stress may have been necessary to lead to the Let-Down Effect, now only slightly elevated states of activation are necessary. Essentially, the body becomes less tolerable and forgiving. This reduced tolerance over time to stress and changes in activation states is called **Sensitization.**

An example of Sensitization in a different context is the case of acquired allergies. Acquired allergies develop after multiple exposures to an antigen, such as dust or bee venom. Consider the example of bee stings. It is possible to be stung by a bee on several different occasions and react with nothing more than minor discomfort and skin irritation. Yet if you were to continue being stung through the years, your body can become sensitized to bee venom. Once sensitized, even minute amounts of bee venom can set off what becomes a profound allergic reaction, such as severe swelling and breathing difficulties (anaphylactic shock) or body rashes. The same is true with the Let-Down Effect. After our physical system becomes sensitized to the Let-

Down Effect, Let-Down reactions can occur even without profound shifts in activation levels.

Sensitization also explains why other symptoms that were initially triggered by massive levels of stress begin to arise under only minor activation states. Back pain sufferers, for example, may find themselves more frequently developing pain under conditions that previously never would have triggered a pain episode. If, in the past, a week of stressful work and High Activation led to severe back pain, now only one workday under these conditions could lead to a pain episode.

Sensitization frequently affects those suffering from Chronic Fatigue Syndrome. When Barbara came to see me, she had been suffering from Chronic Fatigue Syndrome for three years. She experienced great fatigue, poor concentration, an occasional low-grade fever, lack of deep or restful sleep, and physical discomfort in her limbs and shoulders. Prior to developing this condition, Barbara had enjoyed working for ten years as a film editor. While editing a film, it was not uncommon for her to work long hours over a series of weeks and months with very little sleep.

Barbara relied on an adrenaline high to keep her energized so that she could complete her projects on time. Once a project was complete, she typically had several weeks to recover before beginning her next film. During this break she usually felt depleted (the Let-Down Effect), and spent much time sleeping and eating more regularly.

After ten years of this routine, Barbara found herself increasingly unable to sustain this work schedule. Her work hiatuses no longer provided adequate recovery time between projects. Her feelings of fatigue began to set in during the course of the film, instead of once she completed it. After a while, Barbara found herself having to turn down jobs due to her fatigue.

Barbara had become sensitized over time to her stressful work conditions. Her threshold for activation had become greatly reduced. Even short periods of activation were capable of triggering Let-Down reactions in Barbara. In essence, she had become an Immediate Reactor. Further, her Let-Down reactions required greater periods of recovery than they had in the past.

With the help of Somafocus, Barbara learned to control her Let-Down reactions. By blocking these reactions, Barbara lessened the fatigue she felt between projects and the recovery time she needed to restore herself. With the help of Limiting Activation techniques (which I will cover in the next chapter), Barbara was able to bolster her body's tolerance for activation.

Although Somafocus helped Barbara regain control of her health, her case is a strong argument in favor of prevention. The sooner you begin using Somafocus to block the Let-Down Effect in your life, the greater are your chances of eliminating the long term consequences of the Let-Down Effect, such as

Sensitization and longer recovery periods.

Chapter 9 Summary:

1. Over time, our body becomes increasingly sensitive to sudden shifts between activation states.

2. This sensitivity can lead to the Let-Down Effect being triggered even when there are less abrupt shifts between activation states.

3. The Let-Down reactions caused by this greater sensitivity can result in extensive recovery periods.

Chapter 10

LIMITING ACTIVATION

Three Techniques

So far, this book's strategy for dealing with Let-Down reactions has focused on the slowing of the transition between activation states. Somafocus accomplishes this by slightly increasing activation levels. In so doing, Somafocus enables us to slow the transition to Low Activation (for the Let-Down Reactor) or to High Activation (for the Delayed Reactor).

This chapter will explore a second way of blocking Let-Down reactions. The goal of this approach is to reduce the amount of High Activation that we feel in the first place. By reducing the amount of High Activation in the body, we can minimize the extent of the drop that occurs as we shift into Low Activation. Diminishing the size of the drop lessens our chances of Let-Down reactions. Unlike Somafocus, which raises activation levels, this approach relies on lowering activation levels.

This method of lowering activation levels is particularly useful for Immediate Reactors, who develop symptoms while in the heat of the stress battle. However, it can be beneficial to anyone who encounters stressful situations and is vulnerable to Activation-related illnesses.

Consider adding any one or all of the following techniques to your daily routine. In as little as one to two minutes a day, these techniques can help you reduce stress and prevent illness. These techniques are also helpful when used at the first onset of symptoms.

Maintaining A Healthy Activation Level

In Chapter 5, you learned to think of activation levels in terms of miles per hour (MPH). To carry this metaphor further, it may be useful to think of the body functioning best over extended periods of time at a certain speed. For example, a car reaches its optimum miles per gallon (MPG) at a specific speed. If it goes beyond this speed, there is a higher consumption of gas and a lower MPG.

Similarly, if our bodies chronically exceed their healthy activation speed, we increase our chances of developing Activation-related illnesses. Let's say, for example, that your body functions best between 50 to 60 miles per hour. This optimum speed is different for everyone; some people do best at 45 MPH, while others may function better at 55 MPH. How do we know when our bodies are moving at a healthy speed? We know we are moving at a healthy speed when we are alert and focused but do not experience negative High Activation indicators, such as tension, restlessness, and physical symptoms related to stress. If we manage to remain healthy over extended periods, then chances are we operating in this optimal speed. Therefore, if we can keep our activation level at or below our critical levels of 50 to 60 MPH, then we have a greater probability of remaining healthy.

Naturally, there are going to be times when we exceed this activation level or speed limit. There may be times when we find ourselves reaching speeds of 80 to 90 MPH. That is not the problem. The problem arises when we continue to average this high speed over extended periods of time.

The goal then is to find a means of keeping our **Average Activation Level (AAL)** during the course of the day below our critical level. We can achieve this goal by using techniques that allow us to have brief breaks or respites during the day. These breaks effectively lower our Average Activation Level and keep it from exceeding the critical level.

How do we know when we've reached a critical level? Again, refer to the Speed Table on page 49. Anything from tension and tightness to rapid heartbeat and shallow breathing can indicate that we have reached our critical level.

Fortunately, there are ways of keeping our activation at more moderate and healthful levels. I will describe three techniques that you can use to lower your activation level below the critical threshold.

Remember, it is not necessary to keep your Activation Level below the critical level on a constant basis. Instead, it is important that your body receive respites that enable it to ultimately average a lower activation level across the course of an entire day. In this manner, your **AAL** remains below the critical level. By remaining below this threshold, you can lower the likelihood of developing symptoms.

Technique 1: The Breath Technique

I developed the Breath Technique as a tool I could teach to hospitalized patients who were in an acute state of stress. I had tried a number of other breathing and relaxation exercises throughout the years to relax these types of patients. But many times I found that it took too long for these exercises to take effect or that patients found them too cumbersome to continue on their own.

Determined to find another approach, I connected myself to a number of biofeedback monitors that could monitor my heartbeat, blood pressure, and respiration levels. Over a number of trials, I was able to devise an easy technique that rapidly induced a state of relaxation and significantly lowered blood pressure and heartbeat.

I have found that sometimes in as little as 45 seconds, this technique can substantially shift an individual who is in an acute state of stress to a state of relaxation. Over the ten years that I have been using this technique, it has been over 95% successful. Due to its ease of use and rapid effect, the Breath Technique is an effective tool to lower activation levels. It requires only a minimal amount of time, generally one to two minutes to a make a difference. By sprinkling this tool several times across your day, you can make a substantial difference in lowering your AAL. It is best applied at your first awareness of your activation level staring to spike.

Sit comfortably with your feet on the ground and your back straight. Place your hands on your lap, with either your palms facing each other or facing upward. You can do this exercise with your eyes opened or closed. If you find yourself in a highly stressful and noisy environment, try to find a quiet space to do the exercise, such as another room, the restroom, or even your parked car.

Step 1:   **The Inhale**

1.   Inhale through your nose while your mouth is closed. Take a <u>slow,</u> deep breath for three to five seconds.

2.   Inhale in a comfortable way. Do not inhale to such a degree that your chest feels overly expanded and tight. Do not elevate your shoulders or overly emphasize diaphragmatic breathing.

3.   Place your sense of physical attention on your chest or your head – not on your stomach or legs.

4.   Imagine a sense of lightness or wholeness in your body — as opposed to your body feeling that it is separated by parts.

Step 2:   Holding the Breath

1.   After completing your inhale, hold your breath comfortably for 2 to 3 seconds

Step 3:   The Exhale

1.   Place your tongue behind your top front teeth while your lips are slightly parted.

2.   Gently exhale a small amount of air through your lips — but not through your nose. Your exhale should make a "thhh" sound.

3.   Do not inhale. Wait one to two seconds, and make a second exhale.

4.   Do not inhale. Wait one to two seconds, and make a third exhale.

5.   Following the third exhale, slowly release

the remaining air in your lungs. However, do not deplete yourself of all the air in your lungs.

Step 4:   **Repeat Steps 1 through 3**

1.   Do the exercise four to six times in a row. It will take approximately one to two minutes.

Questions:

1.   After completing the Breath Technique, do you feel a lower activation level?

2.   Is your heart beating slower?

3.   Do you feel a pleasant lightness or calmness?

Using the Breath Technique two to three times a day brings the best results. If you are under particular stress or experiencing extended periods of High Activation, then use the technique more frequently. Typically, applying the technique in the earliest stages of High Activation will prove to be the most fruitful.

After consistently using this technique for a period of a few weeks and months, you will likely notice that you have reconditioned yourself to react differently to stress. You may find that situations that previously led to a critical level of activation no longer have that effect. More important, you will have managed to keep your AAL below the critical levels that lead to Activation -related illnesses.

Technique 2:   The Hand-Warming Exercise

The goal of this exercise is to warm the skin temperature of the palm of your hand. The temperature of your palms can range from 78 to 98 degrees Fahrenheit. This broad spectrum of possible temperatures enables you to easily modify the heat of your hands with your mind.

In acute stress, your body moves the blood from the periphery (hands, feet, etc.) to the central (chest) part of the body. Thus, during stress (High Activation), your hands become colder. By warming your hands, you are slowing activation, preventing this redirection of the blood flow from occurring, and thereby neutralizing some part of the body's stress response.

Sit comfortably on a chair with both feet on the ground. Place your hands on each thigh. Gently close each hand in a relaxed fist. Imagine one of your hands becoming warmer.

There are several ways to do this:

1. Imagine holding a warm cup of tea or coffee. Feel the warmth of the cup permeating your hand.

2. Imagine running warm water over your hand from a faucet. Or, think of placing your hand in a hot bath or Jacuzzi.

3. Imagine passing your hand over a warm toaster or oven.

4.   Imagine holding a warm potato and feeling waves or pulsations of warmth move from the potato into the palm of your hand.

As you do the exercise, feel the warmth in your hand continue to build and spread across your entire palm. Be patient as you wait for these sensations to develop. They may develop quickly, or it may take five minutes before you notice a change. Does the warmth start to spread to other parts of your hand, such as the fingers and the top or outer part of your hand?

Next, place the hand that you have been warming on top of your other hand. Do your hands feel like they are different temperatures?

If you are unable to warm your hand at all, try sitting on the palm of your hand. Once your hand begins to feel warm, place it back on your lap as before. See if you can sustain the warmth. Can you warm it up even more?

Use the Hand-Warming Technique as you would

the Breath Technique. It is a quick way to lower your activation to safer levels and below the critical AAL threshold.

Technique 3: **Popping the Question**

In some cases, asking yourself two simple questions can be enough to take the edge off of your activation level. If you should find yourself consistently exceeding your healthy AAL, then ask yourself the following two questions (assume you have been racing at 80 MPH, which exceeds your healthy AAL of 60 MPH):

1.   Can I still be productive and effective if I move at 60 MPH instead of 80 MPH?

2.   What is more important, my health or traveling at 80 MPH?

Initially, some of us who are caught up in an 80 MPH situation might answer "No" to the first question. Yet, the answer to this question, should nearly always be "Yes." Through conditioning, we have come to expect that extra High Activation is necessary to be productive. In reality, very high levels of activation may actually hamper our ability to be productive. Our "Yes" response to the second question affirms our commitment to our health rather than to potential dangerous and addictive levels of High Activation.

These questions create an awareness that we may have some choices in the present situation. They also remind us that we have some control over our physical and emotional reactions to the present situation. Often, it is the perception that we lack control in a situation that leads to chronically unhealthy activation levels. Control, even if it is an illusion, helps create a more healthy emotional distance and a more healthy activation level.

Chapter 10 Summary:

1. An additional way of blocking Let-Down reactions is to reduce the amount of High Activation that we feel in the first place.

2. When our Average Activation Level (AAL) chronically exceeds critical levels, we increase our chances of developing Activation-related illnesses and symptoms.

3. The goal is to keep our Average Activation Level (AAL) during the course of the day below our critical level.

4. There are three techniques we can use to help us keep our AAL below this critical level.
    A.   The Breath Technique
    B.   The Hand-Warming Technique
    C.   Popping the Question Technique

Chapter 11

WHEN ALL ELSE FAILS:
RESISTANCE TO HEALTH
(When the Mind Interferes with the
Desire to Become Well)

There are times that even with our best efforts to get well, we still find ourselves becoming sick or unable to heal. If you have found, after reading this book, that you could not sustain the improvement of your symptoms or that your symptoms showed no improvement, then there are several factors to consider. First, you may be one of the individuals who is, for whatever reason, less responsive than others to Somafocus. In general, I have found that 80% of the people who use Somafocus can effectively alter their physical responses. Second, your condition may not be one that responds to Somafocus. Third, there could be other factors that are interfering with your attempts to heal. This third possibility will be the focus of this chapter.

In 1993, I published a study that was conducted at Cedars-Sinai Medical Center in Los Angeles. This study was part of the Psychoimmune Program, which I had founded and directed. This program used such strategies as hypnosis and visualization to help medical inpatients and outpatients heal faster or modify their physical symptoms. Patients were referred to my program for a variety of different medical problems, including cancer, heart disease, autoimmune disorders, and chronic pain.

One hundred and twenty patients participated in the study. All of these patients were hypnotized, and while under hypnosis were asked if it was acceptable to them to become well.

Of these 120 patients, an astounding 40% said "No" to becoming well. I refer to this phenomenon as **Resistance to Health**. Although the presence of this resistance was generally not what had caused these individuals to become sick, it was sabotaging their efforts to heal.

When we first develop a physical symptom or illness, it can be due to a physical complication in the body that is not caused by stress. For example, we can develop a concussion headache caused by an automobile accident or a severe case of gastritis triggered by something we ate. If the symptom becomes chronic, the mind begins to develop a line of communication to this part of the body. For most individuals, this communication network was not there prior to the physical condition. However, once we crystallize this network, aspects of the mind, such as emotions and thoughts, become capable of affecting this symptom or condition. In short, the mind develops the power to either make the symptom worse or make the symptom better.

In certain cases, our emotions have a **hidden agenda**. The purpose of this agenda is to accomplish certain ulterior goals that we feel unable to accomplish in more direct or healthy ways. The symptom then becomes a means of fulfilling this mental or hidden agenda. In essence, the mind begins to use the physical condition as a tool to deal with or avoid dealing with other aspects of our lives. Therefore, we develop a resistance to giving up this symptom, since it serves an important function. This is the root of what I call **Resistance to Health**, a dynamic that can interfere with our best efforts to heal.   There are four main Resistance to Health themes in which the mind uses an illness as a tool to carry out its hidden agenda: Nurturance, Withdrawal, Punishment, and On–the–Hook.

Nurturance Resistance to Health

There are two types of Nurturance Resistance to Health. In the first, the mind uses the symptom or condition to force us to slow down and take better care of ourselves. This situation often occurs in those individuals who have been under significant stress of some kind, and the mind cannot justify slowing down. The illness then becomes the justification for taking the time the body needs to feel better.

An example of this condition was an attorney who came to see me for help in dealing with his irritable bowel condition, which was causing him to experience bloating, cramping, and diarrhea. He typically worked 60 to 70 hours a week. However, since he developed this condition, he was being forced to reduce his work schedule .

All of his efforts to heal had failed. He had tried a number of medications, nutritional changes, acupuncture, and herbs – all without success. We learned, through our work together, that his mind believed that if he were to become well, he would again return to a hectic and unhealthy lifestyle. If continuing his illness was the only way to prevent this from occurring, then his mind was determined not to loosen its grip on his stomach. He only began to heal once he committed to a more healthy work schedule, and then remained committed to it once he returned to work.

Our unconscious mind is motivated by safety, and if it lacks a healthy way of creating safety, it will come to rely on illness as a means of creating safety.

Questions:

1. Do you find it difficult to slow down or relax?

2. When you get sick, is that generally the only time when you nurture or take care of yourself?

   If you answered "Yes" to the above, then you run the risk of an illness or a symptom becoming part of a mental agenda that forces you to nurture yourself.

Solution: Your health will depend on your making a commitment to living a healthier life and to doing those things that are supportive of health. This could include more reasonable work hours, adding more joy to your life, or giving yourself more time to sleep and rest.

In the second type of Nurturance Resistance to Health, the mind depends on the symptom as a means of getting attention or nurturance from others. It happens in those individuals who either have difficulty asking for attention or who only receive attention from others when they are sick. This type of Resistance to Health will interfere with healing, since getting well would mean giving up attention or love.

Questions:

1.   Do you find it easy to ask for attention or love?

2.   When you ask for attention or love, do those around you respond to these requests?

3.   Do you feel deserving of attention or love?

Solution: Your ability to heal depends on your ability to ask for attention in a direct way. If the people around you cannot accommodate your requests, develop new networks of friends who can attend to your needs even when you are healthy. Develop a sense of deserving and worth that does not depend on illness.

Withdrawal Resistance to Health

Withdrawal Resistance results when we rely on our symptoms as a means of withdrawing from commitments or responsibilities. The illness allows us to avoid facing areas in our lives that have been disappointing or unfulfilling, such as relationships, career, or financial issues. Focusing on the illness allows us to truthfully say, "Since I am sick, I do not have the time or energy to deal with these other issues."

A chief administrator of a local hospital, named Sandra was referred to me by her pulminologist (a physician who treats lung disorders) for her asthma condition. Her doctor felt that her asthma was being aggravated by psychological issues. I learned that Sandra seldom had any difficulties breathing during the work Primarily, her breathing difficulties began on Friday afternoons. Her difficulty in finding her breath forced her to remain at home during the weekend and interfered with her ability to see friends or accept dates.

Through our discussions, I learned that Sandra had a series of disappointments in her past relationships with men. In her last two relationships, she had been engaged to be married, only to have each end fruitlessly. She harbored great anger and hurt over these losses. It became clear to me that Sandra's asthma had become a way of protecting her from being hurt again in the future. But what a price she was paying for this protection!

Questions:

1.   Is there an area in your life, such as a relationship or career issue, in which you feel frustrated or lack fulfillment?

2.   Do you ever feel subtly relieved that your illness or condition has to take priority over these other unfulfilled areas of your life?

3.   Do you ever find yourself upset that you are

starting to feel better? Or, if you do start to feel well, do you find that you are reluctant to call friends, get out of the house, or get work done?

Remember, the unconscious mind is motivated to create safety. *If there are major areas of frustration in your life, hidden agendas will crystallize to protect you from these issues. If you are ill, these agendas will then ensure that the illness remains the most important distraction or impediment in your life.*

Solution: By allowing illness to be an escape from dealing with the frustrating aspects of your life, you are undermining your chances of healing. It is important that you do not view your illness as an escape or a break from these frustrations. Instead, remind yourself that despite the frustrating nature of these issues, you do not need this sort of protection from them and can instead deal with them in a direct manner. Do your best to remain engaged in life, and commit to attending to the issues in your life – even if you are ill.

Punishment Resistance to Health

In this form of Resistance to Health, we begin using our illness as a way of punishing ourselves. We may believe that we once did something wrong in our lives that deserves punishment.

Robert had been diagnosed with colon cancer, and he continued to work long hours, disregard his health, and miss important medical treatments. As a result, his physician referred him to me. We learned through hypnosis, that when Robert was a child, his father blamed him for his mother's illness. Robert's mother died from colon cancer. Now that he had been diagnosed with the same condition, he felt that he deserved it. Being sick was his punishment for making his mother sick. Therefore, he had come to feel undeserving of treatment that could improve his health.

Questions:

1. Do you ever feel that you deserve to be sick? Have you ever felt that you do not deserve to be happy or healthy?

2. Do you ever find yourself doing things that make yourself sicker, such as eating unhealthy foods or doing what you had been advised not to do by your doctor?

Solution: Consider making peace with old hurts or mistakes that you have made. As long as you continue to feel anger and guilt about such events you leave yourself vulnerable to the possibility that these negative feelings will find ways to punish you with illness.

On–the–Hook Resistance to Health

In this type of Resistance to Health, we use our illness or condition to punish someone close to us, because we feel that person has wronged us. By remaining ill, we continue to punish that person for his or her wrong doing. To heal would mean that we were letting this individual off–the–hook for what he or she did to us.

Margaret came to me after developing Fibromyalgia, a disorder characterized by physical aches, stomach upset, and fatigue. This disorder developed soon after she learned that her husband had an affair. Margaret's husband felt tremendous guilt about the affair and also felt responsible for his wife's disorder. In my work with Margaret, we learned that she was not willing to heal. By healing, Margaret would be letting her husband off the hook for what he had done to her. Only by remaining sick could she continue to punish him.

Questions:

1. Do you find yourself chronically angry with someone you are close to in your life?

2   Do you become angry at this individual if he or she suggests that you are feeling better?

3.   Do you find yourself not wanting to let this person know when you are feeling well?

Solution: It is important that we not use our health as a way to punish others or make a point. We need to assert our needs and feelings in more direct and healthy ways, rather than using our health to do so.

Some More Ways of Recognizing Resistance In Yourself

1.   Do you ever find yourself becoming defensive or argumentative when someone close points out that you appear to be feeling better?

2.   Do you ever find yourself not wanting to let others know that you are feeling better?

3.   Do you find that it is easier to talk about

being ill than it is to talk about being healthy?

4. If you are in the hospital, do you ever find yourself trying to justify to yourself or your doctor why you need to remain in the hospital?

5. Once you begin to feel better, do you find that you start to feel depressed and resistant to resuming previous activities?

6. Once you resume your previous activities, do you find that you begin to feel sick again?

7. Do you look for reasons to justify taking your medications, even if you are actually feeling better?

8. Do you find it difficult to talk about subjects other than your health?

9. Do you find that if you tell yourself that you are not going to get sick or that your pain is going to lessen, that your condition

actually becomes worse?

10.   Do you find yourself becoming ill as you undertake activities associated with anxiety or stress?

If you believe you suffer from Resistance to Health and cannot work through this on your own, you may find it helpful to have a consultation with a health professional who specializes in this area. Generally, those professionals who specialize in Health Psychology and Behavioral Medicine could be of help to you. These professionals could design a strategy to help you overcome these resistances.

Chapter 11 Summary:

1.   In some cases, there may be a part of us that interferes in our ability to become well. When this occurs, it is called Resistance to Health.

2.   These resistances to health develop when our mind has a hidden agenda. The purpose of this hidden agenda is to accomplish certain goals that we feel unable to achieve in more direct and healthy ways. The mind uses illness as a means of carrying out this agenda.

3.   There are four main types of Resistance to Health:

      a.   Nurturance: The mind uses illness as a way of forcing us to slow down and take care of ourselves, or as a way to get attention from others.

      b.   Withdrawal: Illness becomes the means of withdrawing from commitments and responsibilities.

c. Punishment: The mind believes we are deserving of illness as a punishment for some past wrongdoing.

d. On-the-Hook: Being ill is a means of punishing someone close to us.

Chapter12

LET-DOWN IN THE WORK PLACE

I have written this chapter for business owners with employees and for managers of companies. If you are not an employer or in management, you might prefer to skip this chapter and proceed to Chapter 13.

Activation-related illness is a common and costly occurrence in the workplace. The new global economy and greater competition has led to increased work hours and demands being placed on employees. The resulting stress is now affecting a younger level of employee than that of previous generations.

Did you know that:

Several studies have determined stress to be a factor in 60% of all medical visits. The International Labor Organization (ILO) recently reported that one in ten office workers in Britain, the United States,

Germany, Finland, and Poland suffer from some form of stress.

According to the World Federation for Mental Health, stress disorders are increasing to such a degree that by 2020, they will surpass AIDS and violence as the leading causes of loss of work due early death and disability.

The ILO further stated that the costs related to stress disorders run higher than those attributable to plant shutdowns or strikes (Reuters, 10-11-2000).

The costs and risks of employee illness have never been greater. Therefore, employers and employees that can control Activation-related illnesses gain the edge over those who cannot. The companies who ignore or do nothing to control these costs may ultimately compromise the company's bottom line. In today's Wall Street economy, this can translate in lower stock prices and executive salaries.

Initially, those employees who are vulnerable to Activation-related illnesses may develop seemingly harmless conditions, such as colds or flu. These conditions can lead to two to five days of work loss. During the flu season, the Let-Down Effect can significantly increase the number of individuals becoming ill. Of great importance is that individuals can develop more serious Activation-related conditions over time, such as heart disease, chronic pain, hypertension, or rheumatoid arthritis.

Fortunately, it is simple to incorporate Activation interventions in the workplace.

Begin by identifying those employees who have a pattern of illnesses related to activation. Classify them in terms of the three Reactor Types as described in Chapter 4. To review briefly, the three Reactor Types are: the Immediate Reactor, the Delayed Reactor, and the Let-Down Reactor.

The Immediate Reactor becomes sick in the heat of the battle.

The Delayed Reactor becomes ill at the prospect of beginning the next battle.

The Let-Down Reactor becomes sick at the end of the battle.

If you find it difficult to identify those employees who have a history of Activation-related illness in terms of these three types, consider asking the employees to classify themselves. Refer to the questions in Table 3, page 43, for help.

It may also be helpful to observe how your employees handle such stressors as deadlines, stressful projects, conflicts with coworkers, discipline, or performance reviews. All of these situations are potential precipitants or triggers for Activation-related illness. If you notice any of your employees becoming ill after any of these triggers, encourage them to do the exercises that I will describe in this chapter. These exercises, which I refer to as Inoculation Breaks, will help inoculate these employees against future Activation-related illnesses.

Employers or managers who encourage their employees to do these exercises may encounter some resistance. Perhaps the biggest obstacle relates to time. Employees may feel that the Inoculation Breaks prevent them from completing their work. Other employees may feel that the Inoculation Breaks interfere with their momentum or work flow. If you encounter such resistance, it may be helpful to remind your employees that the time lost due to illness will be much greater than the time required for stress inoculation.

It is also important for employees to feel management support for these Inoculation Breaks. If employees cannot do these exercises in their offices or cubicles, consider identifying certain locations where employees can go instead. This could be a vacant conference room, their parked cars, or a quiet office cafeteria.

We will now discuss the different intervention strategies for dealing with the three Reactor types.

Immediate Reactor

The Immediate Reactor becomes sick in the

heat of battle. At work, this generally would mean getting sick while in the throes of a stressful project. Typically, the Immediate Reactor's illness results in the loss of several days of work. However, the loss of several work days can become significant, as it may lead to costly delays and greater pressure on fellow employees to carry the additional workload. This increased workload heightens the chances of other otherwise healthy employees becoming ill, which further compounds the price tag of Activation-related illness. See Table 7.

Delayed Reactor

The Delayed Reactor manages to remain well during the stressful event and even while on vacation. For the Delayed Reactor, the most vulnerable period for illness is actually when he or she returns from a break or a vacation to begin a new a new project or resume a heavy workload. As a result, the Delayed Reactor may come back to work after a vacation merely

Table 7
STRATEGIES FOR THE IMMEDIATE REACTOR

1.   Have the employee identify those trigger events likely to result in stress related illness.
2.   Implement either of the three Limiting Activation Techniques (Chapter 10) several times during the work day, particularly during identified trigger events. This may seem interruptive, but is far less interruptive than several days of absences.
     a.   Limiting Activation exercises will take no more than 2 to 5 minutes a day.
3.   In lieu of the Limiting Activation Techniques, have the employee listen to relaxing music for 5 minutes several times during the work day.
4.   Have the employee listen to a Let Down Prevention CD/Tape several times during the work day.

to return home due to illness. This can result in additional absences from work or compromised work work performance until the employee recovers.

The Delayed Reactor becomes ill due to the rapid shifting from Low Activation to High Activation. By slowing the transition from Low to High Activation, it is possible to minimize the chances of illness. See

Table 8.

Table 8
STRATEGIES FOR THE DELAYED REACTOR

1. Have the employee identify those trigger events, such as returning from vacation, that result in Let-Down related illness.

2. Suggest to the employee that he or she begin using Somafocus (see Chapter 6) at least 2 to 3 times a day, beginning the last day of his or her break or vacation, or no later than the first day back at work. This creates a more gradual shift to higher activation levels.

    a. Each application of Somafocus will generally require only five to seven minutes.

3. Adjust the employee's work schedule for his or her initial return to work. Consider making that initial schedule less demanding or hectic. This allows for a more gradual shift to High Activation.

The Let-Down Reactor

The Let-Down Reactor becomes ill due to a rapid shift from High to Low Activation. It is not

Table 9
STRATEGIES FOR THE LET DOWN REACTOR

1.   Have the employee identify the events or times that he or she is most vulnerable to the Let-Down Effect; such as after conflicts, vacations, weekends, or after completing projects.

2.   Suggest to the employee that he or she begin using one of the Somafocus techniques described in Chapter 6 immediately following these trigger events. It may be necessary to allocate special time during the work day for the employee to do this.

    a.   Somafocus will generally only require 5 to 7 minutes.

    b.   This will slow the transition from High to Low Activation.

3.   Suggest to the employee that he or she consider using one of the Limiting Activation Techniques (Chapter 10) during trigger events in order to lessen the extent of High Activation

    a.   Lowering the amount of High Activation the employee experiences in the first place is another way of lessening the abruptness of the transition from High to Low Activation.

    b.   Limiting activation exercises may take as little as 2 to 5 minutes a day.

necessary for Let-Down Reactors to go on vacation in order to become ill. They can become ill after finishing a stressful project at work, after a conflict with a coworker or their boss, or on a Friday afternoon. Let-Down illnesses tend to worsen with time, in that lesser amounts of stress and activation become capable of creating illness. Consequently, more frequent and extensive absences begin to materialize as Let-Down reactions remain untreated. See table 9.

Chapter 12 Summary:

1. Activation-related illness is a common and costly occurrence in the workplace.

2. The employer may want to identify those employees who are most vulnerable to Activation-related illnesses. Involve the employee in this process.

3. Classify the employee in terms of three categories:

   a. Immediate Reactor

   b. Delayed Reactor

   c. Let-Down Reactor

4. Each reactor type has specific strategies for overcoming Activation-related illness.

5.. The biggest obstacles to these health strategies relate to time, employee and management's perception of work interruption, and management support.

6. The time lost due to Activation-related illness is often greater than the collective time required for Inoculation Breaks.

Chapter 13
WHAT'S NEXT?

By learning the tools that prevent the Let-Down Effect and other Activation-related illnesses, you now have the ability to assume far more control over your health. Your increased sensitivity of activation levels gives you an expanded awareness of your body. This heightened awareness increases your chances of being able to promptly intercede in the chemical chain of events that can lead to illness in the body. In the same way that an "ounce of prevention is equal to a pound of treatment," early intervention in the Let-Down process increases the odds of your success.

Somafocus and the Limiting Activation exercises give you tools to alter your activation levels. Not only can this ability help prevent Activation-related illnesses, it can also benefit you in other ways as well. With increased experience in using these techniques, you may find that certain activation levels are best for the successful accomplishment of specific tasks.

For example, you may learn that you problem solve best at an activation speed of 60 MPH (characterized by an alert, active mind), while an activation speed of 65 MPH (alert and energetic, "up" and absorbed) is most effective for public speaking. Since Somafocus and the Limiting Activation Exercises enable you to alter your activation levels, with practice you will be able to use these techniques to place you in the proper zone that is optimum for your performance.

It is most important, however, that you be patient with these techniques, for it takes time to become proficient. Also, be careful to avoid having unrealistic expectations, such as assuming that you can stop all illness with these techniques. Rather, be realistic and take a moderate position. If you can improve your odds of remaining well by 50 to 70%, then this is significant. Few medical interventions can boast a 100% success rate.

Modern medicine will continue to evolve and develop new treatments for conditions previously not treatable. Yet despite the future gains in medicine, there will always be conditions that medicine cannot successfully treat. As a result, future treatment will place greater emphasis on the role that the mind plays in creating health. Health interventions will increasingly use the mind to create the internal chemical states that bolster and increase our chances of healing. New arsenals of mind techniques will be developed as part of a new health technology.

Somafocus and the Limiting Activation Exercises are part of this new health technology. What you have learned in this book represents the future course of healthcare. By using these techniques in your life, you have an opportunity to be part of this ongoing and evolving new health technology. Although this new technology cannot assure us that we will never be ill again, it will substantially increase our odds of remaining healthy. Equally important, is that this new health technology has the capability of significantly enhancing the quality of our life.   When traditional medicine reaches its limits, this new arsenal of health technology can allow us to move beyond these limits in ways that further embellish our health, happiness and well-being.

Quick Order Form

Fax Orders:	818-880-0607
E-mail Orders:	marcschoen.com
Phone Orders:	866-624-2665 (toll free)
	(866-MBH-BOOK)
Postal Orders:	Mind Body Health Books
	P. O. Box 8579
	Calabasas, CA 91372

Name:_____

Address:_____

City_____State_____Zip_____

Telephone_____

E-mail address_____

Please send the following:

Item	Price	CD/T	Quantity	Total
Book	$19		_____	_____
Let Down Prevention CD	$12	____	_____	_____
Healing CD	$12	____	_____	_____
Sleep CD	$12	____	_____	_____

All CDs are available on Cassette Tape

for the price of $12 - **please specify CD or T (tape)**

Sub Total	_____
Tax***	_____
Shipping**	_____
Total	_____

***Sales Tax : California residents add 8.25% to all orders

**Shipping:

US: $4.75 for the first book and $2.00 for each additional book

or CD/Tape. $2.00 for each CD/Tape.

Payment: Check_____   Credit Card___

Visa___Master Card___

Card Number:_____

Name on card_____Exp_____

Signature_____

154

Quick Order Form

Fax Orders:	818-880-0607
E-mail Orders:	marcschoen.com
Phone Orders:	866-624-2665 (toll free)
	(866-MBH-BOOK)
Postal Orders:	Mind Body Health Books
	P. O. Box 8579
	Calabasas, CA 91372

Name:_____

Address:_____

City_____State_____Zip_____

Telephone_____

E-mail address_____

Please send the following:

Item	Price	CD/T	Quantity	Total
Book	$19		_____	_____
Let Down Prevention CD	$12	____	_____	_____
Healing CD	$12	____	_____	_____
Sleep CD	$12	____	_____	_____

All CDs are available on Cassette Tape

for the price of $12- **please specify CD or Tape(T)**

Sub Total	_____
Tax***	_____
Shipping**	_____
Total	_____

***Sales Tax : California residents add 8.25% to all orders

**Shipping:

US: $4.75 for the first book and $2.00 for each additional book

or CD/Tape. $2.00 for each CD/Tape.

Payment: Check_____ Credit Card___

Visa___Master Card___

Card Number:_____

Name on card_____Exp_____

Signature_____

Quick Order Form

Fax Orders:	818-880-0607
E-mail Orders:	marcschoen.com
Phone Orders:	866-624-2665 (toll free)
	(866-MBH-BOOK)
Postal Orders:	Mind Body Health Books
	P. O. Box 8579
	Calabasas, CA 91372

Name:_____

Address:_____

City_____State_____Zip_____

Telephone_____

E-mail address_____

Please send the following:

Item	Price	CD/T	Quantity	Total
Book	$19		_____	_____
Let Down Prevention CD	$12	____	_____	_____
Healing CD	$12	____	_____	_____
Sleep CD	$12	____	_____	_____

All CDs are available on Cassette Tape

for the price of $12- **please specify CD or Tape (T)**

Sub Total		_____
Tax***		_____
Shipping**		_____
Total		_____

***Sales Tax : California residents add 8.25% to all orders

**Shipping:

US: $4.75 for the first book or disk and $2.00 for each additional

book or CD/Tape. $2.00 for each CD/Tape.

Payment: Check_____   Credit Card___

Visa___Master Card___

Card Number:_____

Name on card_____Exp_____

Signature_____

158

Dr. Schoen is a Licensed Clinical Psychologist and has been on staff at Cedars-Sinai Medical Center since 1983. He was the founder and Director of the Psychoimmune (Mind-Body) Program at Cedars-Sinai Medical Center, one of the first of its kind in the country.

He is an Assistant Clinical Professor in the School of Medicine at UCLA, where he teaches hypnosis in the medical school and conducts research in the field of Mind-Body Healing or Psychoneuroimmunology. Dr. Schoen is also on Cedars-Sinai's Teaching Faculty in Psychiatry where he teaches hypnosis to the psychology and psychiatry residents and fellows.

Dr. Schoen has a private practice in Beverly Hills, California. Since 1983, he has focused his practice on helping his patients learn to use their minds to positively affect their health. Dr. Schoen has been featured extensively in the Los Angeles Times, Wall Street Journal, and other publications, as well as interviewed by major televison and radio networks.